NEVER FAR
FROM GRACE

NEVER FAR
FROM GRACE

Rosalie Haffner Lee

Review and Herald® Publishing Association
Washington, DC 20039-0555
Hagerstown, MD 21740

Unless otherwise noted, Bible texts in this book are from The New King James Version. Copyright © 1979, 1980, 1982, Thomas Nelson, Inc., Publishers.

Texts credited to NIV are from the *Holy Bible, New International Version*. Copyright © 1973, 1978, International Bible Society. Used by permission of Zondervan Bible Publishers.

Bible texts credited to TEV are from the *Good News Bible*—Old Testament: Copyright © American Bible Society 1976; New Testament: Copyright © American Bible Society 1966, 1971, 1976.

Scripture quotations marked NASB are from the *New American Standard Bible,* © The Lockman Foundation 1960, 1962, 1963, 1968, 1971, 1972, 1973, 1975, 1977.

This book was
Edited by Gerald Wheeler
Designed by Bill Kirstein
Cover Illustration: Harry Anderson / Photo inset: Joel Springer
Type set: Times Roman

PRINTED IN U.S.A.

95 94 93 92 91 90   10 9 8 7 6 5 4 3 2 1

R&H Cataloging Service
Lee, Rosalie Haffner
  Never far from grace.

  126 p.

  1. Bible—O.T.—Samuel—Study.   2. Salvation.   I. Title.
                                   224.5

ISBN 0-8280-0604-0

Dedication

This book is lovingly dedicated
to my husband, Ken,
my mother,
and my sister, Carol,
who encouraged and supported me
in the writing of it
during a time of personal transition,
and illness, and crisis within our family.

Introduction

The book of Samuel records a difficult period in Israel's national life. It was a time of change and political unrest as the often weak leadership of the era of the judges came to an end and Israel faced the invasion of what historians call the Sea Peoples. The Sea Peoples belonged to a massive migration from the areas of the Aegean Sea and what is now known as modern Turkey down along the eastern coast of the Mediterranean. The Egyptians barely prevented them from invading their own homeland. One of the Sea Peoples, the Philistines, presented a constant menace to the Israelites, either through military conquest or the more subtle danger of friendship and cultural assimilation.

The tribes of Israel, loosely bound together in a kind of confederacy, had no central government. Their history as the chosen people and their worship of Yahweh were the strongest ties that held them together, and when these bonds weakened, Israel's existence as a nation hung in the balance.

The book of Samuel (1 and 2 Samuel comprised one book in the ancient Hebrew manuscripts) opens with the birth of Samuel the prophet, who will bridge the transition from the time of the judges to that of the kings. His birth answers a mother's sincere prayer, and she names him "heard of God" or "asked of God."

Though he dies before the end of the account, the whole book is really his lengthened shadow. Obviously compiled at least sometime after the death of Solomon, it presents a vivid account of the last of the judges and the new monarchy under Saul and David. But the book of Samuel is more than just a historical account of Israel as a nation. The story of people —real people with real problems— it unfolds a drama of varying temperaments, complex relationships, and paradoxical characters.

We see people caught up in the great conflict between good

and evil. Good people who at times succumbed to the forces of evil both within and without. Promising people who invited failure and ruin by prostituting their God-given powers. Self-serving people whose conduct often affected whole families and even their nation.

First and second Samuel tell how real men and women coped with the forces that still plague us in our world of sin. Some of the accounts will encourage us, others will repel or even disgust us, but all of them will help us better understand the cause and effect relationship of sin in the terrible conflict between good and evil that all of us are engaged in.

The choices made by the men and women in the book of Samuel determined their ultimate destiny. The importance of those choices we see illustrated in the birth of two babies, one near the beginning of 1 Samuel, the other toward the middle of 2 Samuel.

Ichabod arrived on the scene at a moment of national catastrophe. His dying mother named him Ichabod ("Alas for the glory") to remind her people that indeed "the glory had departed from Israel" because of the prevailing evils under Eli's weak leadership. Failure to make right choices had brought national disaster and ruin.

Later in 2 Samuel another baby entered the world as the result of a tragic mistake by Israel's greatest leader. The unnamed son died because of his father's sin. Then a second son came from the same union. The king named him Solomon, but the prophet countered with another name—"Jedidiah, because of the Lord" (2 Sam. 12:25, KJV). The name, meaning "Beloved of the Lord," provided assurance of redemption and forgiveness in spite of the king's sin and bad choices.

The narratives in Samuel herald the good news of the gospel in Old Testament garb. They remind us that in our human frailty and weakness we are no match for the enemy. But they should also encourage us to believe that no matter how far we fall or how deep our wounds, we are never far from God's grace and mercy—if we choose to respond to Him.

With the psalmist we may claim the Rock as our fortress,

our strength, our deliverer. His Saviour can be ours, rescuing us from the enemy who wants to destroy us. But thank God, salvation is ours if we will but choose it. Each of us may become "Jedidiah, beloved of the Lord."

Contents

1

When Everyone's Doing It

CONDITIONS IN ISRAEL

Imagine what life would be like if our nation had no constitution or central government, and everyone did his own thing. Consider what it would be like if an enemy controlled our country's whole coastal region, and unfriendly nations regulated strategic cities and transportation routes.

How secure would we feel in time of war if we had no armed forces to depend on other than a volunteer army hastily put together without training or much organization?

Such were the conditions in Israel when the story recorded in the book of Samuel begins. It covers a period in Israel's history when the enemy of God and man seemed determined to wipe His covenant people from the face of the earth.

The long period of the judges had been a difficult time for God's people. Inclined to a peaceful farming life, they were ill-prepared to meet military and political challenges from their neighbors.

The 12 tribes had no central government, and when a crisis arose, the Israelites had to depend on voluntary help from the various tribes, which might take considerable time to assemble. The rugged terrain of some parts of Palestine, plus the formidable barriers of certain strategic cities (such as Jerusalem) and the Plain of Jezreel, still in the possession of the Canaanites, hindered cooperation between the southern and northern tribes.

Some of the northern tribes, especially those near the coastal regions, often entered into trade coalitions with the Canaanites, thus making it politically untenable for them to fight against their spiritual enemies. A case in point appears in the Song of Deborah, which remonstrates with Dan and Asher for failing to aid Deborah and Barak against Jabin, king of Hazor (see Judges 5:16f.).

But even more threatening was Israel's attraction to Baal and other Canaanite gods. Often the worship of Baal and Yahweh merged into each other. The Israelites called themselves worshipers of Yahweh, but absorbed the rituals, customs, and ideology of their pagan neighbors. Such theological confusion often led to outright idolatry. The biblical record says repeatedly, "They forsook the Lord and did not serve Him. So the anger of the Lord was hot against Israel" (Judges 10:6, 7). David Payne, commenting on such spiritual adultery, says, "There is plenty of folk-religion, embodying pagan superstitions, still prevalent within Christendom despite the availability of churches and copies of Scripture." [1]

With the lack of strong leadership among the judges, "everyone did what was right in his own eyes" (Judges 21:25). It seemed that Satan would succeed in his attempt to destroy God's chosen people before they could accomplish their mission of representing Him to the nations.

WANTED: A GOOD MOTHER

But when things look the darkest, God often sends a ray of light, sometimes a guiding star in the night. Israel required a strong spiritual leader to turn the tide, and God needed a woman who could produce such a man.

When God wanted a Moses to lead His people out of Egypt He found a Jochebed to prepare him. To produce a John the Baptist to prepare the way for the Messiah, He selected Elizabeth. And when He needed a human mother for His own Son, He chose Mary.

Now He found Hannah to give Israel a leader who would establish them as a nation and bring in a new era. Married to Elkanah, a Levite from Mount Ephraim, and childless, she had endured the frustration and agony of being a rival wife. Polygamy always created problems and unhappiness, shattering the peace and harmony that should exist in a marriage.

Holidays and special occasions also produce extra tensions in strained relationships. And this family dilemma was no exception. Elkanah loved Hannah, and even though she had borne him no children, on the occasion of the national feast he gave her a special portion of the sacrifice to show his devotion to her. But the gesture only inflamed the jealous Peninnah. Her taunts and provocations cut deeply into Hannah's sensitive nature. She might have blamed her husband or nagged him to get rid of her cantankerous rival, but instead Hannah did what every child of God should do when vexed and grieved: she "prayed to the Lord and wept in anguish" (1 Sam. 1:10). Her prayer was not a selfish, vindictive lashing out against her envious rival. Rather it was a vow that expressed her faith in the ultimate triumph of right over wrong. If only God would grant her request for a child, she would dedicate him back to God for life.

Eli's comment, "How long will you be drunk?" (verse 14), shows the condition of Israelite society even among those worshiping at the tabernacle. Drinking was part of Canaanite rites and may have crept into Israelite worship. The priest's command, "Put your wine away from you" (verse 14), followed by the mention of intoxicating drink, intimates that God did not approve of alcohol of any kind or of drunkenness among His people.

Samuel was the product of Hannah's suffering. Suppose she had not been barren, thus had not pleaded for a son or vowed to give him to God for life? Israel might never have had a prophet and leader to guide it through one of its most crucial periods of national life.

Scripture does not record the agony that must have wrenched Hannah's heart when she took her baby to the tabernacle to live with strangers. Did she tremble at the thought of the evil influence of Eli's family? Did she wonder what kind of woman would have responsibility for her young child? (Probably one of the women who served at the tabernacle according to 1 Samuel 2:22.) Nor does Scripture mention the lonely days, weeks, and months that both mother and son must have endured between those cherished annual visits when she would bring a little robe to the budding young priest. It comments only that "the child Samuel grew in stature, and in favor both with the Lord and men" (1 Sam. 2:26), suggesting that she had done her work well.

During those few short years that she nurtured him, she shaped the future of her people. Perhaps she knew by instinct what child specialists now confirm, that the first three years of a child's life mold its entire personality, emotional frame, and character. The hand that had rocked his cradle would indeed influence Israel for many years to come. "From the earliest dawn of intellect she had taught her son to love and reverence God and to regard himself as the Lord's." [2]

Hannah's paean of praise for God's answer to her request is one of the most beautiful songs in Scripture (1 Sam. 2:1-10). Overtones of the great controversy between good and evil permeate the prayer. It points forward to a time when truth and righteousness triumph and the Lord will have broken the bows of the wicked (verses 9, 10). Her song foreshadows the coming of the Messiah, when the horn of God's ultimate anointed (verse 10) would be exalted.

A CRISIS IN LEADERSHIP

The narrator of Samuel now shifts from this beautiful story of simple faith and the fruit of a mother's love and devotion to the contrasting account of Eli and his sons. The terse note, "the sons of Eli were corrupt; they did not know the Lord" (1 Sam. 2:12), suggests much to our imagination. Privileged and pampered by their indulgent father, they had grown up believing that their status as priests gave them license to whatever they wished. The high priest failed in his duty to discipline his strong-willed sons as young children, and now his peace-loving nature shrank from exercising the authority he knew was his obligation. As he witnessed their rebellion and immorality—some of it probably in imitation of Canaanite fertility worship—he was appalled, yet he recoiled from taking action against their corruption.

"They did not know the Lord" (verse 12). Although brought up in a priest's home, exposed from infancy to the sacred services, they did not have a personal experience with Yahweh.

They viewed Him in the same way as did the Canaanites around them. What a tragic commentary on Hophni and Phinehas, who might have become great leaders in Israel had they chosen to know God, had they seen in the sanctuary service a path to the very heart of God instead of primarily a way to manipulate Him.

But their self-indulgence eventually led to skepticism and even rebellion against the sacred services of the sanctuary. During the peace offerings, the fat was to be burned upon the altar (see Lev. 3:3-5, 16), then the worshiper gave a certain portion of the meat to the priest, and his family was to eat the rest as a symbol of gratitude and faith in the great Sacrifice to come. But Eli's corrupt sons would force the sacrifice from the offerer before the proper steps had been taken, thus bringing contempt on the whole service in the eyes of the worshipers.

God patiently warned Eli of the consequences if he did not restrain his evil sons. But dreading the public disgrace such a course would bring, and fearing his sons' reaction, he excused their behavior and allowed them to continue their profligacy.

The Covenant God of Israel is a God of mercy *and* justice. The book of Samuel stresses both the idea of redemption and deliverance (as illustrated in the birth of Samuel) and the concept of judgment (as seen in the example of Eli and his sons). As one Bible commentator puts it: "Judgment-within-love permeates both Testaments." [3]

An unnamed prophet warned Eli that both his sons would die for their sins, and God's honor would be eventually vindicated. "Then I will raise up for Myself a faithful priest who shall do according to what is in My heart and in My mind. I will build him a sure house, and he shall walk before My anointed forever" (1 Sam. 2:35). Later during Solomon's reign, the prophecy came to fulfillment when Zadok replaced Abiathar, the descendant of Eli, as the high priest. [4] The line of Zadok would minister for centuries to come.

Perhaps an even more significant aspect of the prophecy is that Samuel, who served as Israel's prophet, priest, and judge, was a type of the One to come who would be their prophet, priest, and king. Samuel's grandson, Heman, was one of David's leading musicians, and as such exercised the prophetic as well as the Levitical gift (1 Chron. 6:33; 25:4-6). In a sense Samuel, both in his own right and as a type of Christ, fulfilled this prophecy.

A CALL AND A CHOICE

"The word of the Lord was rare in those days; there was no widespread revelation" (1 Sam. 3:1). God depends on human agents through whom He can communicate His will. When few are willing to be His prophetic voice, the spiritual condition of His people worsens. Such was the world that the boy Samuel grew up in.

Evidently the aged Eli found great comfort in the spiritually sensitive child. Perhaps he saw in him what he wished his own sons could have become. In spite of the priest's tragic failure and the disgrace it brought upon Israel's religious life, he carefully nurtured the child's spiritual life.

God was grooming Samuel for leadership. The child's life at the tabernacle provided him an education in divine service, as well as lessons in how not to lead.

Then one night "before the lamp of God went out in the tabernacle of the Lord where the ark of God was" (verse 3), young Samuel, lying down to sleep, heard a voice calling his name.

Why did God's voice sound like Eli's to him? Perhaps because in spite of his failures, the aging priest was still Israel's leader. Samuel recognized Eli's voice as the highest human authority in his life. Do we see here a lesson for God's children today? Our spiritual leaders often exhibit weaknesses and human error, but they are still God's appointed ministers. They are His voice on earth, and God requires that we respect and reverence them.

Samuel's ready response, "Speak, Lord, for Your servant hears" (verse 9), has become a model for children and youth. His willing choice to answer the summons to become a spokesperson for God has inspired many a boy or girl to follow his or her Saviour's call. A call to service, perhaps a call to sacrifice home, friends, and family to travel to some faraway region to give his or her life in unacclaimed devotion. Perhaps a call to be faithful in some lowly task. Or to go beyond the normal demands of duty in some great undertaking.

Samuel's choice to answer meant delivering an unpleasant message. It meant risking the priest's approval and acceptance. Today responding to God's summons may compel us to leave the comforts of home and loved ones to share God's love with the repulsive and unappreciative. It may mean persecution, even death.

Making his decision, Samuel "told him everything" (verse 18), whatever the consequences. And that choice led to additional ones, "so Samuel grew, and the Lord was with him and let none of his words fall to the ground" (verse 19). His reputation as a man of integrity, as well as a prophet, became established in Israel.

Shiloh once again became known as the place where God appeared to His prophet, and where the people could look for guidance and direction. A new day had dawned.

---

[1] David Payne, *Kingdoms of the Lord* (Grand Rapids: Wm. B. Eerdmans, 1981), p. 7.

[2] E. G. White, *Patriarchs and Prophets,* p. 572.

[3] James D. Newsome, Jr., *Commentary on First and Second Samuel* (Atlanta: John Knox Press, 1982), p. 24.

[4] See *The SDA Bible Commentary,* vol. 2, pp. 637, 638.

2

Ichabod or Ebenezer?

HARD TIMES IN SHILOH

While God nurtured and prepared a prophet in Shiloh to minister to His people, the crisis in the priesthood there continued to worsen. If Hannah had produced a Samuel, the record remains silent as to what maternal influence or lack of it may have contributed to the evil course of Eli's sons.

But whatever the reason—genes, home environment, parental influences—the sons of Eli headed down the path of self-indulgence and rebellion at a frightening speed. Their behavior brought consternation to an indulgent father and finally exhausted the patience of a merciful God.

The pleas and entreaties, the warnings of a loving, compassionate God, had gone unheeded, both by Eli and his corrupt sons. Instead of repenting, they actually became hardened in impenitence because of God's delay in punishing them. [1] Disgracefully they used the sacred office to flaunt their licentious and immoral practices before a disgusted and indignant congregation.

Many people became so disillusioned with the priests' behavior that they came to despise and neglect the sacred services that God had instituted. As a result of the irreverence of the priests, confidence in religion waned, distrust in leadership abounded, and spirituality died.

"The work of God was so profaned and dishonored before

the people, that no expiation could be accepted for them. Their own father, though himself high priest, dared not make intercession in their behalf; he could not shield them from the wrath of a holy God. Of all sinners, those are most guilty who cast contempt upon the means that Heaven has provided for man's redemption." [2]

A TIME FOR JUDGMENT

How much longer would God allow the mockery and insult to Himself and the destruction of the faith of His children to continue? God had warned that when the day of accounting came it would be so evident that people's ears would tingle (1 Sam. 3:11). The sins of a nation and its leaders had made it ripe for the judgments of God, [3] and He now allowed their most wily enemy to be the instrument for that judgment.

The formidable Philistine army, camped in Israelite territory, no doubt hoped to penetrate the hill country and eventually gain control of the center of Israelite life at Shiloh. As an agrarian people, the Israelites were ill-prepared to face the fierce Philistines with their iron weapons and expertise in war. The very first skirmish dealt a deadly blow to the poorly organized forces of the 12 tribes. The elders met in emergency session. What should they do?

Perhaps because spirituality was at such a low ebb, the Israelite leaders failed to recognize their fundamental source of help. Instead of seeking guidance from their divine Commander in Chief, they took matters into their own hands.

The elders concluded that if the sacred ark accompanied their forces, surely the enemy would be defeated (1 Sam. 4:3, 4). It was a widespread belief in the ancient world that a nation's god or gods accompanied the army into battle. An invisible supernatural conflict waged in each war. Thus many viewed their idols as possessing some magical charm that—if present with their military forces—would protect them. Regarding the ark of the covenant as a talisman, the people of Israel now believed that its physical presence would save them—even though they had acknowledged that God had deliberately allowed the Philistines to defeat them (verse 3). Why would they think He would change

21

His mind now? But they were determined to make Him fight for them.

When the sacred chest entered the camp, they shouted so loudly that it seemed the very earth shook (verse 5). The Philistines, upon learning that the ark had arrived, at first responded in terror. Soon, though, their leaders challenged them, "Be strong and conduct yourselves like men" (verse 9), and fight they did. Israel suffered a stunning defeat with great casualties. But the most terrifying calamity of all was that Israel's most powerful enemy had captured the ark of God.

News of the dreadful defeat reached the home front quickly. Eli, now an old man, broken in spirit by his evil sons, fearful for the future of his nation, and laden with anxiety and guilt because he had allowed God's people to carry the sacred ark into battle, waited with trepidation. The news of the death of his sons did not take him by surprise, but the fate of the ark of the covenant was too much for the aged priest.

Imagine the horror and anguish that must have filled his heart. He knew that his sin had dishonored God and caused Him to withdraw His presence from Israel. The thought was more than he could bear. His strength gone, he fell from his position on top of the wall by the gate "and his neck brake, and he died" (verse 18, KJV). [4]

Eli's pregnant daughter-in-law, the wife of Phinehas, upon hearing the news, went into labor. The death of her husband and father-in-law, and especially the tragedy of the ark, sent her into a state of shock. Evidently a godly woman though married to the wicked priest, she shared Eli's concern for the spiritual welfare of the nation. As she died in childbirth, she requested that her child be named Ichabod, saying, "The glory has departed from Israel, for the ark of God has been captured" (verse 22).

SIGNIFICANCE OF THE ARK

God had instructed Moses to place the sacred tables of God's commands from Sinai into the ark beneath the mercy seat. "And there I will meet with you, and I will speak with you from above the mercy seat" (Ex. 25:22). The glory of the infinite God condescended to meet man there. "The holy Shekinah, the visible manifestation of Jehovah's presence''[5] revealed the divine majesty to humanity.

Why then had the ark in their midst not brought victory to Israel? The sacred ark, containing the Ten Commandments, served to remind them of God's requirements for them as His covenant people. As long as they lived in harmony with the divine requirements contained there, God would be their protector and defense. But disobedience had brought separation from God. They had grieved the Spirit of the Lord from among them. [6]

Instead of recognizing the ark as the very dwelling place of God, they came to see it much as the pagan nations viewed their idols—as possessing some magical charm in and of itself. The ark became a talisman. But even worse, they thought of it as a way to manipulate God to their will.

The ancient religions believed that the gods needed man to build homes for them to live in (the temples and shrines) and to feed them (the sacrifices and offerings). Consequently, humanity had power over their gods and could to a certain extent force them to do their will. Israel began to think of Yahweh in the same way. If they took the ark—His footstool and dwelling place —into battle, He would fight for them. But their misunderstanding of its significance made the ark no less sacred, as the ensuing events demonstrated.

Many Christians make a similar mistake today. Some become legalists because of their misunderstanding of how to relate to God's holy law. Others in their zeal for truth focus on doctrinal beliefs as though they in themselves can bring salvation. Still others allow liturgy, rites, and ceremonies to become the essence of their religious life.

But the law is still a revelation of God's character even though some in their misunderstanding become legalists. Doctrine is no less God's will unfolded despite the fact that some focus on it instead of who it reveals. Liturgy as an expression of worship, a means of bringing us closer to God, should not be disposed of because some make it an end in itself. The story of the ark reminds us not to lose sight of the true significance of that which God has entrusted to us. Nor should we despise the sacred symbols because some misuse or misunderstand them.

SHORT-LIVED TRIUMPH

The Philistines were elated to think that they had captured "Israel's god." Clearly, since they had defeated Israel's forces, they had defeated Yahweh. Now they would demonstrate that fact to all in the land. Bringing it to the house of Dagon, their national god, they supposed it would combine with his power to make them invincible. But their elation and hopes were short-lived.

Dagon, a name coming from a Semitic root (*dgn*) having to do with clouds and rain, was apparently a fertility god, probably a grain god. But Yahweh, the Lord of Israel, had not been defeated, and He—the true source of all life—now demonstrated His power. He had let the Philistines capture His ark for a purpose.

Entering their temple the next morning, they found the statue of their god mutilated and fallen on its face (1 Sam. 5:3). But even more distressing, the people of Ashdod suffered a deadly disease (verse 6).

The ark made the rounds to the major Philistine cities, each time with the same results. For seven months it remained in enemy territory, bringing plague and distress to each city that it was taken to. The Philistine rulers were convinced that the curse of Israel's God must be upon them (verses 7-12).

According to pagan custom, the Philistine priests directed the people to send the ark back to Israel with appropriate peace offerings, shaped according to the specific plagues that had afflicted them. Each replica of a tumor (Hebrew '*opel*) represented a major Philistine fortified city or acropolis. To test Israel's God, the Philistine leaders suggested that two cows, whose young calves were to be left behind, should pull the rough wooden cart with its thick wood wheels. If indeed the cows returned to Israel, against their natural inclination, the Philistine leaders would be sure that Israel's God was to blame for the disasters they had suffered (1 Sam. 6:1-9).

THE ARK RETURNS

Guided by an unseen hand, the two cows headed straight for Beth-shemesh, the nearest Levite city (verses 10-12). The arrival of the ark amazed the men of Beth-shemesh and filled them with joy. But instead of seeing its miraculous presence as a call to repentance and revival, they treated the sacred chest with mere human curiosity and wonder (verses 13-15).

God's judgment against the men of Beth-shemesh was swift and severe (verses 19, 20). The people of Israel had been taught to reverence the sacred ark. Even the Levites were not to look on it. The Philistines had apparently had more respect for it than the men of the Levite city. The inhabitants of Beth-shemesh did not bother to consecrate any priests to care for it.

Some Hebrew manuscripts omit the words "fifty thousand" in verse 19. Judges 6:15 translates the word for thousand as family. Thus the record might more accurately read "and he smote among the people 70 men of 50 families." [7]

Still the terrible tragedy, instead of leading the people of Beth-shemesh to repentance, filled them with superstitious fear and a desire to get rid of the sacred ark as soon as possible (verse 21). The men of Kirjath-jearim responded to the invitation to take the ark, and it abode in the house of Abinadab, a Levite, until David would find a home for it many years later.

Tampering with the symbol of God's divine presence had taken a high toll, both in Israel and among the Philistines. The birth and naming of Ichabod, a son of the priestly family, had highlighted the tragic failure of God's people to be a light to the world as the glory of God's presence dwelt among them. The glory had departed for a time. Now with the ark returned, God awaited an opportunity to reveal His glory and renew His covenant relationship with His people once more.

EBENEZER: STONE OF HELP

That opportunity was not long in coming. With the death of Eli, Samuel now became the recognized leader of the tribes of Israel. His first official act was to lead the people in a spiritual revival. His call for them to "return to the Lord with all your hearts" followed with a passionate appeal to reformation: "put away the foreign gods and the Ashtoreths from among you, and prepare your hearts for the Lord, and serve Him only" (1 Sam. 7:3).

Samuel gathered the people together at Mizpah for a day of fasting and prayer. Confession of sin, destruction of their foreign gods, and renewal of their vows to God followed.

The Philistines, though they despised Israel's weakness, feared the strength of their God. Hearing of the revival taking place under Samuel, they gathered their forces quickly and marched to battle against God's people at Mizpah. Remembering their earlier defeats at the hand of their enemy, the Israelites, panic-stricken, implored Samuel to pray for them: "Do not cease to cry out to the Lord our God for us, that He may save us from the hand of the Philistines" (verse 8).

The biblical record states that Samuel offered a burnt offering, and "cried out to the Lord for Israel, and the Lord answered him" (verse 9).

God's response was dramatic. He sent a storm against the people who worshiped Dagon, the son of the storm god Baal Haddu, and "thundered with a loud thunder . . . and so confused them that they were overcome before Israel" (verse 10). Perhaps thinking that their own Baal, the storm god, was fighting against them, they fled in terror.

Israel gained a stunning victory that day. They recovered much of the territory the Philistines had taken from them, some of the enemy strongholds surrendered, and Philistine hostility to Israel weakened for most of Samuel's administration.

Such a victory demanded celebration. "Then Samuel took a stone and set it up between Mizpah and Shen, and called its name Ebenezer, saying, 'Thus far the Lord has helped us' " (verse 12).

Israel had failed miserably when they depended on their own wisdom and resources. Now they had enjoyed the fruit of total dependence on God. Samuel did not want them to soon forget the experience. The Ebenezer stone would constantly remind them that only in the Lord could they safely trust.

"We have nothing to fear for the future, except as we shall forget the way the Lord has led us, and His teaching in our past history." [8]

Ichabod or Ebenezer? We may insist on having our own way, we may disobey and rebel, and ultimately we will pay the price of separation from God and the loss of His glory and presence.

His love and mercy seeks to spare us from such an ordeal, but the choice is ours!

Inviting us to an Ebenezer experience, God pleads with us to repent and return to Him. He calls His church to revival and reformation. We too may set up a memorial, a stone of help, that declares, ''Thus far has the Lord helped us.''

---

[1] *See Patriarchs and Prophets*, p. 582.

[2] *Ibid.*, p. 580.

[3] *Ibid.*, p. 583.

[4] *Ibid.*, p. 585.

[5] *Ibid.*, p. 349.

[6] *Ibid.*, p. 584.

[7] *The SDA Bible Commentary*, vol. 2, p. 478.

[8] *Testimonies*, vol. 9, p. 10.

3

When the Church Clamors for Conformity

SAMUEL, THE IDEAL LEADER

In many ways the portrait of Samuel as Israel's ruler represented God's ideal for a human leader under a theocracy. The Lord had called and trained him from childhood for his position. As a peace-loving man, with apparently no military ambitions for himself or his nation, he committed his energies to the spiritual interests of his people. A man of prayer and close communion with his God, he served effectively as priest and intercessor for the people of Israel. Yet he had the ability to exercise the judicial office as well as the political leadership necessary to hold the 12 tribes together.

The period of the judges had been a time of turmoil and defeat, partly because so few leaders had been able to accomplish that bonding that Israel needed to survive as a nation. Now Samuel's ministry provided a transition from that difficult era to a new kind of leadership. For in addition to being a priest, judge, and political leader, he was also a prophet. Though Scripture calls Abraham and others up to that time prophets, Samuel was in a special way the founder of what we know as the prophetic office. His great strength lay in his unwavering trust in God as the true leader in Israel. As he saw the spiritual needs of the nation, he initiated reforms that influenced Israel for years to come.

THE SCHOOLS OF THE PROPHETS

And those reforms came about through education. Samuel established what Ellen White referred to as the schools of the prophets, no doubt his greatest contribution to the nation of Israel. While the term *schools of the prophets* does not appear in the Old Testament, Scripture does clearly imply their description and function. The young men who attended the schools became known as "sons of the prophets" (see 2 Kings 2:3-5), though they did not necessarily exercise the prophetic gift. Rather, God called and trained them to be spiritual teachers to instruct the people in His will.

Samuel established the first such school at Ramah, his ancestral home and headquarters (1 Sam. 19:18, 20), and another at Kirjath-jearim, the site of the ark. Later others appeared at Gilgal (2 Kings 4:38), Bethel (2 Kings 2:3), and at Jericho (2 Kings 2:15-22).

"The schools of the prophets were founded by Samuel to serve as a barrier against the widespread corruption, to provide for the moral and spiritual welfare of the youth, and to promote the future prosperity of the nation by furnishing it with men qualified to act in the fear of God as leaders and counselors." [1]

According to Mrs. White, the schools instructed the students in the law of God, in sacred history, and in the arts—sacred music and poetry. Music served an important part in Israel's worship and religious life. In fact, later in David's reign some equated the gift of music with the prophetic gift (see 1 Chron. 25:1-3).

Students also learned skills and practical trades that enabled them to be self-supporting. They understood the dignity of labor. The discipline of work helped to develop character and the gifts given them by God.

The Word of God formed the basis of their study. There they discovered the principles that comprise the very cornerstone of successful living, whether in the nation, the family, or in the individual life. "The Holy Scriptures are the perfect standard of truth, and as such should be given the highest place in education." [2] "As an educating power the Bible is without a rival." [3]

Samuel must have understood, at least in part, that the work of education and that of redemption are really one and the same, that of restoring God's image in man. The glorious destiny God planned for His people could be accomplished only as they allowed the principles taught in the schools to be worked out in their lives.

REJECTION AND DISAPPOINTMENT

Samuel's office uniquely combined the governmental, social, and religious aspects of Israel's national life. He stood as a representative of God to man and man to God. Therefore Samuel would see any spiritual failure of his people or his nation as a failure of his spiritual leadership.

As he neared the close of his ministry the elders came to Samuel with complaints about his sons, whom he had made judges in southern Judah. Nothing could have hurt his sensitive nature more than to have his own sons misrepresent the very principles he had worked so hard to instill in others.

"But his sons did not walk in his ways; they turned aside after dishonest gain, took bribes, and perverted justice" (1 Sam. 8:3).

Had Eli's poor example influenced Samuel to be a somewhat indulgent father? Had he been too busy being prophet, priest, judge, and educator? Or had his sons simply chosen not to follow the example of their unselfish and godly father?

Whatever the reasons, the elders now used their behavior as a pretext for a request that must have caused his heart to sink. "Make for us a king to judge us like all the nations" (verse 5).

He had devoted his whole life and energies to Israel's spiritual interests. His leadership had been impeccable and had made advances both spiritual and political. The nation had prospered under his wise administration. Now this.

Though stunned by the request, Samuel realized that the real motive of the elders was pride and discontent. The demand was not so much against his sons as it was a desire to reflect the society around them. The Israelites wanted all the military might and court pomp and glamour that accompanied kingship in the surrounding nations.

Still the aged prophet could hardly avoid feeling the sting of failure. But he did what every leader and every child of God should do when confronted with rejection or disappointment. The record states simply, "So Samuel prayed to the Lord" (verse 6).

"WE WANT A KING"

Samuel understood the unreasonableness of their request. As a prophet and priest he was all too well acquainted with their perversity, their lack of humility and submission to God's will. He must have grieved deeply that his leadership should soon end with so much at stake.

But God assured him that the real rejection was not against him as a leader, but rather the reign of their divine King. Egypt and other major powers of the ancient Near East were fading in power, and in their place were rising a number of powerful smaller kingdoms, and the Israelites wanted to join them. Now was their chance to assert themselves on the international scene, and they needed a well-organized government and military force to do it. The voluntary arrangement of the 12 tribes had clearly not worked in the past. Too often different tribes had refused to come to the aid of the others.

It was not the first time Israel had wanted a monarchial ruler. During Gideon's judgeship they had tried to make him king, but he had declined, reminding them that it was the Lord who was to rule over them (see Judges 8:22, 23). A few years later his son Abimelech did accept the invitation of the Shechemites to be their king. His short reign over them ended in tragedy (see Judges 9:7-22, 50-57).

Some Bible scholars believe that the monarchy was a part of God's intentional plan and that Samuel was simply a reluctant old man unwilling to make changes or let go of the reins of government. But because the Lord had given instructions regarding a monarchy does not mean that it was in His divine plan anymore than His provision for the plan of salvation meant that He intended for sin to exist. Knowing the weaknesses of sinful human beings, He simply had a plan B in case it was needed.

God's disapproval of the request was evident. He reminded Samuel that their evil course now was nothing new. For "since the day that I brought them up out of Egypt, even to this day . . . they have forsaken Me and served other gods'' (1 Sam. 8:8).

SAMUEL REVEALS THE COST OF A MONARCHY

Then God said in effect to Samuel, Look, give them what they want, but "solemnly forewarn them" (verse 9) of the high cost of having their own way. Our compassionate and great God lets His people make mistakes rather than coerce the human will. But He does not give His reluctant permission without sufficient warnings as to the consequences of such choices.

Samuel then outlined in rather vivid detail a picture of monarchial government. Had the people believed him they would have fallen to their knees, pleading for God to forgive them for their foolish request. But like so many of us, they heard only what they wanted to hear and blocked out the rest. God had given His reluctant permission, and that was all that mattered just then.

And what were Samuel's warnings and concerns? First of all, he made it perfectly clear that in choosing a king they would exchange their freedom for serfdom. "He will take your sons. . . . He will take your sons and daughters. . . . He will take the best of your fields, your vineyards, and your olive groves, and give them to his servants. He will take your menservants and your maidservants . . . and put them to his work. . . . And you will be his servants" (verses 11-17).

The prophet and judge reminded them that under a monarchy they would be subject to military conscription and high taxation. He warned them of the dangers of the misuse of power, and of forced labor and oppression to satisfy the greed and pride of unscrupulous rulers. Samuel must have cautioned them that in choosing a king they would lock themselves into a system that they could not change at will. The elders seemed to forget that if the priest's sons could be vile and the prophet's sons dishonest, the king's sons could be corrupt. Kingship would pass on by birth, not by worth.

"And you will cry out in that day because of your king whom you have chosen for yourselves" (verse 18). How often throughout the centuries of the monarchy that prophecy would be fulfilled.

But choosing a king with all of the inherent hazards was not Israel's greatest folly. The real tragedy lay much deeper: "You have today rejected your God, who Himself saved you out of all your adversities and your tribulations" (1 Sam. 10:19). Indeed, they had spurned God's authority, His divine leadership, His power to protect them from their enemies. Instead of trusting Him they chose to place their faith in human might and prowess.

In spite of the warnings that having a king would not be in their best interest, the Israelites persisted in their determination to be like the nations around them. "The people refused to obey the voice of Samuel; and they said, 'No, but we will have a king over us'" (1 Sam. 8:19).

"The longing to conform to worldly practices and customs exists among the professed people of God. . . . Christians are constantly seeking to imitate the practices of those who worship the god of this world. Many urge that by uniting with worldlings and conforming to their customs they might exert a stronger influence over the ungodly. But all who pursue this course thereby separate from the Source of their strength." [4]

Upon the occasion of the confirmation of Saul as Israel's new king, Samuel again reprimanded them for their rejection of God as their leader (1 Sam. 12:17). Already they sensed that they had greatly erred. In bitter remorse they cried out to Samuel, "Pray for your servants to the Lord your God, that we may not die; for we have added to all our sins the evil of asking a king for ourselves" (verse 19).

The prophet's response evidenced a genuine concern for the people he loved even though they had seemingly rejected his own leadership. "Far be it from me that I should sin against the Lord in ceasing to pray for you" (verse 23). With a true shepherd's heart he acknowledged his duty as a spiritual leader to continue holding up his people before the Lord even though they had sinned.

Samuel in his intercessory ministry foreshadowed our great High Priest who "ever lives to make intercession" for us (Heb. 7:25). The prophet carried the burden of his people's sins, but Jesus actually "bore our sins in His own body on the tree" (1 Peter 2:24). Although Samuel spoke words of encouragement to his people, "Do not fear" (1 Sam. 12:20), Jesus could say, "Be of good cheer, I have overcome the world" (John 16:33). And "Lo, I am with you always, even to the end of the age" (Matt. 28:20). Samuel promised to teach the people the right way (1 Sam. 12:23), but Jesus proclaimed Himself to be "the way, the truth, and the life" (John 14:6).

CHOICES: CONFORMITY OR CONFESSION?

The people of Israel faced choices: to conform to the world or to obey God. To insist on having their own way or to seek divine leading. To refuse reproof or to accept rebuke and turn to God with confession and repentance.

We today also have similar decisions to make: to conform to worldly standards and customs, thus ignoring God's will, or to accept God's principles as outlined in His Word. To refuse to recognize that we have all too often rejected God's leadership and gone our own way, or to admit our failures and return to Him with genuine repentance. To neglect our great High Priest, or to come to Him daily with our confessions, accepting His wonderful intercessory work in our behalf. The choices are ours. The results will reach into eternity.

---

[1] *Patriarchs and Prophets*, p. 593.
[2] *Education*, p. 17.
[3] *Patriarchs and Prophets*, p. 596.
[4] *Ibid.*, p. 607.

4

When God Gives a New Heart

DESTINY AND CHOICE

I srael has asked for a king, and God has given His reluctant permission—but not without conditions. Israel's monarchial system must differ from that of the surrounding nations. God Himself will choose their king.

The first eight chapters of the book of Samuel have focused on the ministry of Samuel the prophet. Now the narrative shifts to the often complex and intricately woven story of Israel's first two kings. They were two men whose lives and destinies seemed paradoxically opposite at almost every point. The contrasts will be evident throughout the narrative. So much so that if it were not for the part of the story we are about to consider in this chapter, one would be tempted to believe that the saga of Saul and David proves that God predestines some men to a certain fate which nothing, not even their own choice in the matter, can change.

Those who espouse absolute predestination believe that God "immutably wills the salvation of the elect" and the destruction of those not elected. [1]

Did God favor David, and later Solomon, above Saul? Or did all of them have equal opportunities in the monarchy as well as personal salvation? Did God foreordain each of them to an inevitable fate, or did their own deliberate choices make the difference in their ultimate destinies?

For all their diversity, contrasting characters, and varied

temperaments, both men had one thing in common: each began his career as a good man, and each had a personal encounter with God. How they chose to nurture and continue their spiritual life fills the pages of the remainder of the book of Samuel.

Saul's entry onto the stage of Israel's new venture unfolds with a hint of royalty. His pedigree, listing five generations (representing at least a century), implies that his family was of some prominence and prestige. His father, Kish, was a wealthy farmer (the word translated "power" in 1 Samuel 9:1 in the original Hebrew suggests a man of influence and power in his community who had extensive possessions). [2]

But the record quickly informs us that Saul's greatest asset was his regal bearing. Handsome, and in the prime of life, [3] he stood tall, head and shoulders above his peers. "He appeared like one born to command." [4]

Though God had reserved the right to assign Israel's king, He evidently chose one who fit their demands and ideal. Someone who would gratify the pride that prompted them to desire a king in the first place. [5] Someone they could look up to, someone who could fight their battles for them.

LOST DONKEYS AND A KING FOUND

The complex details of this story reveal several interesting insights about the man whom God chose. Kish sends his son Saul out to look for some lost donkeys. One of his servants accompanies him (only the wealthy could afford servants). They travel many miles unable to find the animals. Finally Saul becomes concerned that his father will stop worrying about the donkeys in his anxiety for his lost son (evidence of close family ties).

The servant suggests they seek the advice of a "seer," or prophet, and willingly offers to pay for the services out of his own pocket. (Why didn't Saul think of going to see the prophet? Is it possible that his Benjaminite family were not overly religious? After all, his ancestors from Gibeah had a somewhat sordid history during the time of the judges [see Judges 20].)

In any case, the fact that we know of no previous connection or acquaintance between him and Samuel highlights the providential meeting that took place that day. Aided by some young women who tell them where Samuel will perform sacrifice, they hasten to catch up with him.

Meanwhile, on the day before Saul's arrival the prophet has received a communication from the Lord that He will send him the man whom he is to anoint as Israel's new commander. As Saul and his servant approach the city, Samuel comes out to greet them.

As the two men meet for the first time, the Lord says to Samuel, "There he is!" (1 Sam. 9:17). The NASB reads: "Behold, the man! . . . This one shall rule over My people."

Saul's search for his donkeys ends in finding the man who will alter the course of his life. And Samuel has encountered the king whom God has chosen in answer to the people's demand.

SAUL ANOINTED

With his assurance that someone has located his father's donkeys, the prophet adds the surprising question "And to whom is all the desire of Israel turned, if not to you and all your father's family?" (verse 20, NIV).

Saul remonstrated with the prophet. "Why do you say such a thing to me?" "Am I not a Benjamite, from the smallest tribe of Israel, and is not my clan the least of all the clans of the tribe of Benjamin?" (verse 21, NIV).

The story leaves much to our imagination. Did Saul know that Samuel was looking for a king? Did he indeed understand the implications of the prophet's words? How did he feel when the cook brought the special portion of the sacrificial meat offering usually reserved for the priest? Why would the first king of Israel be chosen from the small tribe of Benjamin instead of one of the more powerful tribes such as Judah or Ephraim?

Apparently the day's strange events did not keep Saul from sleeping well that night, for the next morning Samuel awakened him, reminding him that he had a special message for him as the new king-designate.

The old prophet then took a clay flask or juglet of oil (probably spiced olive oil), and in an act that every Israelite recognized as a sacred anointing, he kissed him, saying, "Has not the Lord anointed you leader over his inheritance?" (1 Sam. 10:1, NIV).

In the patriarchal system the birthright blessing passed from father to son by the laying on of hands, accompanied by words of approval and acceptance, and sealed with a holy kiss (see Gen. 27:26-29). Samuel now followed a similar procedure as he passed on to Saul his own mantle of leadership. The kiss signified not only his blessing on the new king, but revealed his own spirit of humility in showing affection and acceptance for the man who was about to replace him as Israel's leader.

The rite of anointing was a religious symbol used to set priests aside for holy office. Now God instructed through His prophet that the kingship was not to be so much a secular and political office as a sacred and holy one.

David Payne suggests that in Egyptian culture it was a custom to anoint vassal kings or minor kings who owed allegiance to the great king of Egypt. [6] So the new king of Israel was to be the vassal of Yahweh, their true king.

Samuel must have spent some time giving instructions and explaining the principles upon which the new constitutional monarchy would operate. Imagine the seasoned, experienced prophet, judge, and priest giving a crash course in leadership to this rugged donkey herder who likely had little or no formal education.

The narrative does not take us into Saul's mind, revealing his reactions to his new challenge. It only gives us a few brief glimpses. When Saul returned home, his uncle questioned him about his visit with the prophet. But Saul was careful not to mention anything "about the matter of the kingdom" (1 Sam. 10:16). Did his uncle suspect that his handsome nephew had been chosen as Israel's new king? Had Samuel invoked silence upon him until his public anointing, or was Saul simply modest and a bit embarrassed about the whole matter? Later at his public anointing he actually hid "among the equipment" or baggage train (verse 22), and someone had to search him out to make an appearance.

Whatever strengths and weaknesses Saul may have exhibited, whatever doubts and fears the prophet may have had about the personal qualities of the future monarch, one thing was certain —physical stature and princely bearing would not be enough to fill the sacred office according to God's plan. Saul needed better credentials than a good physique!

CHANGED INTO A NEW MAN

Samuel knew that Israel needed a spiritual leader, a Spirit-filled man, in order to carry out the responsibilities successfully. Being a man of prayer, the prophet must have spent hours interceding on behalf of the new king. And now he sent Saul on his way with the assurance that something unusual awaited him. First, he would find two men who would tell him his donkeys had been found and that his father was worried about him. This served to confirm what Samuel had told him earlier. Second, he would meet three men who would supply him with bread. After all, God is concerned with our temporal needs as well as our spiritual. Third, he would encounter a group of prophets praising God with singing and musical instruments. "Then the Spirit of the Lord will come upon you, and you will prophesy with them and be turned into another man. . . . When these signs come to you, that you do as the occasion demands; for God is with you" (verses 6, 7). God's overtures would demand a response from him. Samuel assured the king-elect that he would know what to do when the time came.

The signs came to pass just as Samuel had promised. Saul did indeed meet the prophets in his own hometown of Gibeah. Moved by the Spirit, he joined in their songs of praise and rejoicing. (The verb form of the Hebrew word used for "prophesy" in verses 6 and 10 does not imply the foretelling of future events but rather the expressing of truth in the form of sacred song. [7])

Music has power to transform hearts and impress divine truth. On this occasion God used music to reach Saul and bring about his conversion. Later in his reign music would once again play an important part in touching his better nature.

Samuel had prayed for the man chosen to be Israel's first king. God had provided His Spirit to bring about the needed change. Now Saul responded by opening his life to the influence of God's Spirit. "God gave him another heart" (verse 9), literally, "changed his heart." Saul experienced a genuine conversion.

The power of the Holy Spirit came upon him as he joined the prophets in worship. He had a new concept of the holiness of God. And with that, he realized his own sinfulness and unworthiness and received courage and wisdom for his new challenge and duties. [8]

Saul's experience astonished the people of Gibeah. "Is Saul among the prophets?" became a proverb among the people.

THE ANOINTING AT MIZPAH

Whatever Saul's reaction might have been to his new role, he followed Samuel's instructions to meet him at the appointed time and place. The prophet and last of the judges called the people together for the public announcement and anointing of their new king at Mizpah.

The prophet reminded them how God had led them out of Egypt, how He had protected them and preserved them as His own. Once again he chided them for rejecting God as their deliverer and for demanding a king to rule over them.

Though God had already designated Saul, Samuel went through the official action of choosing a king by lot. "And Saul the son of Kish was chosen. But when they sought him, he could not be found" (verse 21). The burden of the responsibility before him must have overwhelmed him.

The details of the narrative are dramatic. Someone runs and finds Saul. He appears before them, standing head and shoulders taller than any of them. Samuel introduces him as their new king. Overcome with the emotion of the moment and the charisma of their new commander, they shout, "Long live the king!" (verse 24).

Samuel now reads to them "The Behavior of Royalty" (verse 25, a document on the rights and duties of the king, and instruction on proper conduct of the royal office; cf. Deut. 17:14-20).

The king must be an Israelite by birth. Not multiplying horses, wives, or wealth, he should have humility as the hallmark of his servant-leadership role. And he must observe all the commandments of God, keeping the book of the royal requirements in a prominent place and reading them often.

THE NEW KING SAUL

"And Saul . . . went home to Gibeah, and valiant men went with him, whose hearts God had touched" (verse 26). It had been an impressive debut for Israel's new king. Not only had God's Spirit touched his heart, but he left surrounded by courageous men who shared the same experience. How different Israel's future might have been had Saul chosen to renew his vows to God at every step of his royal journey.

But for now the experience was genuine, as subsequent events demonstrated. Opportunity for Saul's leadership presented itself eventually in the Ammonite siege of Jabesh Gilead (1 Sam. 11:1-6). Rising to the occasion, Saul rallied his forces and rushed to the aid of his fellow countrymen. He earned the respect and loyalty of his subjects by taking command of the situation, and uniting them into action in a crisis. While the majority had welcomed Saul at his public anointing, a group of rebels had opposed him. The people now suggested that the new king punish them. But Saul's answer evidenced his true conversion and his recognition that God Himself was their leader and deliverer: "Not a man shall be put to death this day, for today the Lord has accomplished salvation in Israel" (verse 13).

Saul had proved his ability as commander in chief of Israel's forces. Now the kingdom must be confirmed, this time at Gilgal. The transfer of leadership from Samuel to Saul necessitated a gradual process. Because of the new ruler's inexperience and the need to install a completely new system of government, some time had passed by.

In his farewell address Samuel called the people to witness his own impeccable administration. He reviewed the history of God's patient and forgiving leadership over His people. Once again he reminded them of their rejection of God as their divine king (1 Sam. 12:1-5).

But still he held out hope for the tribes of Israel. In spite of their sin in insisting on having a king to rule over them, God would not forsake them if only they would remain loyal and obedient to His voice.

God confirmed the prophet's words by an act of nature. Rain would be almost unheard of in Palestine at wheat harvest time (verse 17). Palestine has a rainy season extending from October into late March/early April. The rest of the year is dry and it rarely rains. Grain harvest comes after the dry season begins. But by a dramatic and out-of-season thunderstorm God impressed His people with the gravity of their sin and disobedience. They became afraid of both Yahweh and His prophet (verse 18).

The people responded by acknowledging their guilt in asking for a king. Samuel reassured them of God's continuing love in spite of their sin. "The Lord will not forsake His people, for His great name's sake, because it has pleased the Lord to make you His people" (verse 22).

The prophet appealed to Israel to renew their covenant vows to be faithful and loyal to God. He held out the hope that if only they would "fear the Lord, and serve Him in truth with all your heart," God would continue to lead them, "for consider what great things He has done for you" (verse 24).

The church today needs the same hope and encouragement held out to God's ancient people. We too have sinned in making wrong choices. But God does not forsake us. Rather He calls us to obedience and loyalty to His principles. He offers forgiveness if we will acknowledge and confess our guilt. And He desires for us renewal, a daily conversion that we may be new men and women, filled with His Holy Spirit. The choice is ours. As it came to Saul and the people of his day, so it arrives for each of us today.

---

[1] Jerome Zanchius, *Absolute Predestination* (Marshallton, Del.: National Foundation for Christian Education, 1980), p. 13.

[2] Howard F. Vos, *Bible Study Commentary: 1, 2 Samuel* (Grand Rapids: Zondervan, 1983), on 1 Sam. 9:1.

[3] Early in Saul's reign his son Jonathan bravely fought the Philistines. Saul must have been in the prime of life to have a grown son.

[4] *Patriarchs and Prophets*, p. 608.

[5] *Ibid.*

[6] David F. Payne, *Commentary on 1 and 2 Samuel* (Philadelphia: Westminster Press, 1982), p. 50.

[7] *The SDA Bible Commentary*, vol. 2, p. 494.

[8] See *Patriarchs and Prophets*, pp. 610, 611.

5

When Pride Prevails

SAUL QUIT TOO SOON

After the victory over the Ammonites and the coronation service at Gilgal, Saul disbanded his army instead of waging aggressive warfare against Israel's other impending enemies. [1] Perhaps he felt that he had little choice in the matter. Because the Israelites did not have a strong sense of national identity, it was difficult to get them to cooperate even during a crisis (as we see throughout the book of Judges), let alone at a time when danger did not seem so immediately apparent.

The initial request for a king had come as a result of the constant threat of the powerful neighboring Philistines. These "Sea Peoples," who according to Jeremiah 47:4 and Amos 9:7 had come from Caphtor (or Crete), had been pushed out by invaders from their previous homes and were now trying to extend their control of the coastal plain into the hills of Palestine.

As Saul began his reign the wily Philistines had worked their way into Israel's hill territory. Their "garrisons" or command posts in the hill country, such as at Geba, indicate their intent to control the whole area west of the Jordan. (David Payne points out that in a way they succeeded, for we still use the term *Palestine,* derived from their name, to refer to the region to this day.) [2]

The well-organized and highly efficient Philistine fighting machine would have made Saul and his people even more reluctant to take the offensive. The Philistines' iron-shielded chariots with swordlike projections on the wheels, the size of their forces, [3] and their expert military strategy made them a formidable foe.

To make matters worse, the Philistines exercised a monopoly on metal working, including the manufacture of weapons. Every time an Israelite wanted to have a tool sharpened, he had to go to a Philistine blacksmith. (Archaeological analysis of Philistine and Israelite sites indicates that they contained equivalent ratios of metal objects. Also, recent archaeological discoveries have thrown light on the rather obscure statement in the King James Version of 1 Samuel 13:21. Newer translations correctly state that "the charge for a sharpening was a pim," or a two-thirds shekel weight [NKJV].)

Morale ran low as a result of the Philistine threat. Saul waited till the second year of his reign before making plans to subdue the invaders. One of the most difficult passages in the book of Samuel introduces the story. [4]

THE PHILISTINE THREAT

Saul now divided his forces into companies, 2,000 men staying with him at Michmash to guard the main road from Jericho and the Jordan valley, and another 1,000 accompanying his son Jonathan to a lookout point at Gibeah. (Excavations have brought to light what archaeologists believe to be Saul's fortress capital at Gibeah, now known as Tell el-Ful, an Arabic name with the interesting meaning of "mound of beans.")

There the valiant Jonathan attacked a garrison of the Philistines (the Hebrew word for *garrison* could mean either a fortress or more likely a "prefect" or officer). The biblical record does not give Saul's reaction to his son's bravery. Did he feel a sense of fatherly pride? Or did a seed of wounded selfish pride now take root in his heart over the fact that his son—not himself—had acted with courage?

The Philistines rallied immediately with their well-organized forces. Panic stalked through the Israelite ranks. Saul knew he had but little time to rally his frightened men. He also realized that if ever he needed the direction and blessing of the prophet, it was now. Samuel and Saul had agreed to meet at Gilgal to do sacrifice before going out to battle (1 Sam. 13:8). But the prophet's arrival seemed delayed. Terror filled the hearts of Saul's men and many deserted, some crossing the Jordan for safety, others hiding in the caves and pits that abound in that region.

SAUL'S FIRST TEST

The Israelite king's first great testing time had come. Would he patiently rely on God for wisdom and direction? Would he prove trustworthy of the great responsibility placed on him as the undershepherd of God's people? Could he inspire his fainting followers to look to the real source of their strength?

Restless and impatient, Saul now took matters into his own hands. The sacrificial service, designed to point the minds of the people to God's ability to act in their behalf, seemed to him a mere religious ritual, one performed to guarantee success.

Desperate and overwhelmed by the confusion and desertion of his men, Saul now commanded the sacrifice to be brought to him. Equipped with armor and weapons of war, he approached the sacred altar to perform the work God had designated to be done by the priest alone. "What he lacked in real piety he would try to make up by his zeal in the forms of religion." [5] But "real piety begins when all compromise with sin is at an end." [6]

No sooner had he finished than Samuel appeared on the scene. Imagine the anxiety and distress that must have filled the prophet. But even more disappointing was Saul's response to the confrontation between them. Instead of recognizing his mistake and showing a spirit of genuine remorse, Saul now excused his behavior on the pretext of great piety. "The Philistines will now come down on me at Gilgal, and I have not made supplication to the Lord. Therefore I felt compelled, and offered a burnt offering" (verse 12). In essence he had blamed Samuel for what had happened. Israel's new king had failed his first test!

Piety seemed to motivate Saul's actions. How could something that seemed so right be so wrong? The king's reason for presuming to act in the role of priest certainly sounded logical enough. After all, the safety and well-being of his people was at stake. Something had to be done. Why shouldn't he, as Israel's leader, take action in the absence of the prophet?

Saul now listened to the prophet announce his failure. He had acted presumptuously, disqualifying himself for the leadership role God required. The monarchy must rest on the supreme authority of Israel's true King. Consequently God would give the kingdom to one who would honor that principle.

JONATHAN WINS ANOTHER VICTORY

The king remained at his fortress at Gibeah (1 Sam. 14:2). Meanwhile the courageous Jonathan and his armorbearer saw an opportunity for a secret attack against the enemy.

The British general Allenby allegedly used the graphic description of the geography of this encounter to help him take Michmash from the Turks in 1917. [7] Jonathan and his companion no doubt knew the area far better than did the Philistines. By making their way through a narrow ravine up to a sharp precipice, they encountered the Philistine host, possibly at dawn, according to Josephus. [8]

Thinking the rocks and holes were full of "Hebrews," the Philistines panicked. God rewarded Jonathan's faith by sending an earthquake that further frightened the enemy.

Seeing the route of the Philistines, Saul rallied his men and joined the battle. Confusion prevailed in the enemy camp as "every man's sword was against his neighbor" (1 Sam. 14:20). To make matters worse for them, the Israelites who had defected to the Philistine army now turned against them and joined their fellow countrymen.

God worked for Israel that day. What had begun as a seemingly impossible effort on Jonathan's part now brought victory to the nation.

At the first hint of the Philistine retreat, Saul immediately called for his officers to take roll. Discovering that Jonathan and his armorbearer were missing, he next summoned the priest to bring the ark of God (1 Sam. 14:18). The ark was at Kirjath-jearim at this time. The Septuagint—the Greek translation of the Old Testament—suggests that he requested the sacred "ephod," not the ark. It contained the Urim and the Thummim. If the latter is the case, it would indicate that he intended to seek for divine guidance, perhaps to cover his embarrassment that his son had once again accomplished what he himself should have done. But instead of obtaining such divine guidance, he rushed into battle.

Now in a rash impulse, Saul pronounced a curse on anyone who would eat food until evening (verse 24). He thought God would be impressed and obligated by his vow. So determined to be honored for his zeal and to protect his royal reputation and authority at any cost, the king needlessly put his people in jeopardy. Weak and hungry, his soldiers fell upon the spoil of their enemies and devoured the flesh with the blood, violating one of the strict commands of Mosaic law. Jonathan, upon hearing of the curse, saw the whole affair as his father's desperate attempt to protect his own selfish ambition. In addition, the prince himself had innocently eaten some honey to strengthen him in battle.

Though Jonathan had won the victory for all Israel that day, Saul determined that nothing should violate his own authority. Jonathan must die! But the people angrily objected. "God forbid: as the Lord liveth, there shall not one hair of his head fall to the ground; for he hath wrought with God this day" (verse 45, KJV).

Had it not been for their intervention, Jonathan would have died at the hand of the one chosen to protect and preserve his people. They must have felt stirrings of misgiving. "How bitter the thought that he had been placed upon the throne by their own act!" [9]

The remainder of 1 Samuel 14 lists the successes of Saul as a military chief. "So Saul established his sovereignty over Israel" (verse 47). The names of his wife, children, and commanding officer give a brief glimpse into his personal life. Such lists usually appear at the end of the story of any given king. One gets the impression that the narrator wishes the story might have ended here. But Saul must yet face his final test.

ANOTHER CHANCE—ANOTHER CHOICE

Still stinging from the prophet's rebuke, and too proud to admit that he had made a mistake, Israel's king instead chafed that Samuel had treated him unjustly and unfairly. Though he still respected Samuel as Israel's prophet, he harbored resentment toward him, and avoided any contact with him.

Though Saul had failed most of his tests thus far, a loving, merciful Father would give him another opportunity, another test, another choice. When the time had come, the prophet approached the king with a message from heaven.

The Amalekites had filled their cup of iniquity. God had in mercy delayed the execution of their sentence for 400 years. [10] Delayed punishment had not resulted in their repentance. Now their idolatry, immorality, and hatred of God's people had reached a point where it was either Israel or Amalek. God chose to exterminate Amalek for the sake of His chosen people and all who might still respond to His love, including the Kenites, who lived among the Amalekites. Saul was to ''go and attack Amalek, and utterly destroy all that they have'' (1 Sam. 15:3). He was to conduct a holy war for the God of Israel.

Judgment day for the Amalekites, in a sense, would also be judgment day for Saul. Samuel made it clear to the king that the ban on the wicked Amalekites was to be complete. (The Hebrew word translated ''destroy'' implies a holy ban. Anything put under such a ban was consecrated to God, and in actual practice this meant complete destruction. Thus the sacred command to ''utterly destroy'' became a kind of curse or ban on everything that belonged to the Amalekites, whether material plunder or captives. Such a practice is difficult for us to understand today, but was common in the ancient world.) [11]

Saul returned from the battle to celebrate his victory with a monument to himself at Carmel. (Compare the king's attitude toward victory in 1 Samuel 11:13.) When he met Samuel he hailed him with a blessing and with the assurance that he had indeed performed the Lord's command.

But even before the prophet heard the lowing of the cattle and the bleating of the sheep, the Lord had revealed to him Saul's disobedience. Because Samuel loved the king as his own son, the disappointment he felt was keenly personal. Grieved, ''he cried out to the Lord all night'' (1 Sam. 15:11).

Samuel reminded the king of God's explicit instructions. Saul had ample opportunity to admit his mistake, confess his guilt, and ask God's forgiveness. Instead he persisted in self-justification. ''But I have obeyed the voice of the Lord'' (verse 20).

''The people . . .''—they are to blame. They took the plunder that should have been destroyed. Unfortunately Saul had over-stepped himself. If his statement were true, he had witnessed against himself that he had not commanded the respect and obedience of his people. But if, on the other hand, it was not true, then he had violated the sacred trust by deliberate disobedience to God's express command.

Looking him intently in the eye, Samuel charged him to "be quiet" and to listen to God's appraisal of the situation: "When you were little in your own eyes, were you not head of the tribes of Israel? And did not the Lord anoint you king over Israel? Now the Lord sent you on a mission. . . . Why then did you not obey the voice of the Lord?" (verses 17-19).

In spite of the blatant evidence, Saul maintained his innocence. "But I have obeyed the voice of the Lord . . ." And in the next breath, he added, "And brought back Agag king of Amalek" (verse 20).

The prophet's solemn declaration of Saul's pious self-justification touches the very nerve center of true heart religion. What good are burnt offerings and sacrifices if they violate a plain command of God? "Behold, to obey is better than sacrifice, and to heed than the fat of rams" (verse 22).

Later the prophet Isaiah would remind God's people that their iniquity made their sacrifices futile, even an abomination (Isa. 1:10-17). Jeremiah, Joel, Micah, and Amos would repeat the same warning to God's people again and again (Jer. 25:3-9; Joel 2:12, 13; Micah 6:6-8; Amos 5:21-24).

Disobedience, no matter how pious the profession, is open rebellion. And "rebellion is as the sin of witchcraft, and stubbornness is as iniquity and idolatry" (1 Sam. 15:23). Samuel's statement was strong medicine for a king who insisted that he had done God's will. Is it possible that disobedience and rebellion can harden the heart to the point that one actually believes he is doing God's will, when in reality he has become an agent of Satan? If so, Samuel had no choice but to deal dramatically with Israel's king.

Saul had brought back a war trophy in the person of the Amalekite king Agag, a common practice of the times. It had seemed to Saul like the right thing to do. However, Samuel was unimpressed, and later executed the pagan ruler "before the Lord" (verse 33), most likely a ritual form of death.

Only when he heard the fateful words of the prophet, He "has rejected you from being king," did Saul admit, "I have sinned."

But even then, instead of asking God's forgiveness, he implored the prophet to pardon him, indicating that he was more sorry that he had lost face with the prophet than from any genuine sorrow for his disobedience.

Saul begged the prophet to return with him, to honor him before the elders of the people by worshiping with him. Samuel reluctantly did so, but not before reiterating his woeful prophecy, "The Lord has torn the kingdom of Israel from you today, and has given it to a neighbor of yours, who is better than you" (verse 28). The Peril of Pride and Power

The tragedy of Saul's life was not just that he sinned, but that he refused to recognize his own rebellion. Pride blinded him from seeing his sin for what it was. It led him to justify his course, then to persist in refusing to repent of it.

Choosing to rebel against God's directives, he neglected the opportunities given him and resisted the appeals of the Holy Spirit to confess his wrong course of action.

Israel's pride had prompted them to press for a king. God had given them one, furnished him with a new heart, and provided plenty of help from the prophet. But his old nature, hidden deep within, assumed itself, persisted, and finally prevailed. The twin menace of pride and power led to his eventual downfall. The trend began early in Saul's reign with apparently innocent or minor infractions. But it ended in total tragedy and ruin.

---

[1] *Patriarchs and Prophets*, p. 616.
[2] David F. Payne, *Kingdoms of Our Lord* (Grand Rapids: Eerdmans, 1981), p. 20.
[3] David F. Payne, *Commentary*, on 1 Sam. 13:5, p. 63.
[4] The only reference to the length of Saul's reign appears in 1 Samuel 13:1. Commentators have long struggled with this passage, but the most logical explanation is that the words describing the actual number of years of his reign were lost in copying at some point. (For more on the length of Saul's reign, see Appendix.
[5] *Patriarchs and Prophets*, p. 622.
[6] *Thoughts From the Mount of Blessing*, p. 91.
[7] *The SDA Bible Commentary*, vol. 2, p. 515.
[8] *Ibid.*
[9] *Patriarchs and Prophets*, p. 626.
[10] *Ibid.*, p. 628; see also Deut. 25:19.
[11] See *The SDA Bible Commentary*, vol. 2, p. 521.

6

When Giants Threaten

GO, ANOINT A KING

Samuel grieved deeply over Saul's failure. Pangs of disappointment and questions of "Did I do enough to help him?" must have plagued the aging prophet. But God interrupted his mourning with the command to go and anoint a successor to the rejected king. "Fill your horn with oil and be on your way; I am sending you to Jesse of Bethlehem. I have chosen one of his sons to be king" (1 Sam. 16:1, NIV).

Though God had reserved the right to choose Israel's first king, He had actually selected a man who met the demands of the people. "There was not a more handsome person than he among the children of Israel" (1 Sam. 9:2). "He was taller than any of the people" (1 Sam. 10:23).

Now God was about to make a choice that revealed His will for His people. He would appoint one who would understand a little better the true ideal for kingship under the divine kingship. One who, though certainly far from perfect, would be a man after God's own heart.

The prophet protested. "If Saul hears it, he will kill me" (1 Sam. 16:2). The current king, still chafing from Samuel's rebuke and God's rejection of him, would interpret any act as treason that appeared to offer competition for the throne.

But God's instructions were specific. Samuel must take a sacrifice and celebrate with Jesse and his family. Then "you shall anoint for Me the one I name to you'' (verse 3).

By now the prophet had learned to trust God's guidance even when things made no sense to him. So the prophet made his way to Bethlehem. The elders of the city questioned his reasons for visiting their town—they did not want to get caught up in the conflict between their king and the prophet—but he assured them he had come peaceably.

God had appointed the place, Bethlehem, where more than a thousand years later another Anointed One would be born. He had chosen the tribe, the large southern tribe of Judah of whom Jacob had prophesied: ''The scepter shall not depart from Judah . . . until Shiloh comes'' (Gen. 49:10). And He had selected the family of Jesse, grandson of Ruth and Boaz (Ruth 4:21, 22). The children must have listened with awe to the fascinating story of their great-grandmother Ruth. Perhaps the account of her faith and loyalty to Israel's God had inspired and helped to shape their lives.

THE LORD SEES THE HEART

Now the prophet, under God's inspiration, would choose one of the sons of Jesse to sit on the throne of Israel. The narrator dramatizes the scene with vivid detail. The tall, handsome eldest son of Jesse passes before Samuel. He impresses the prophet by his princely bearing. Surely he must be the future king of Israel. In spite of Saul's failure and Israel's disappointment in him as their leader, Samuel knew the people still wanted a ruler who looked regal.

''But the Lord said to Samuel, 'Do not look at his appearance or at the height of his stature, because I have refused him. For the Lord does not see as man sees; for man looks at the outward appearance, but the Lord looks at the heart' '' (1 Sam. 16:7).

Each of the other sons in turn failed Samuel's inspection. Each time God said no, not this one. And each time, it left the prophet puzzled. ''Are there any others?''

''Yes, the youngest. He's out herding sheep.''

''Bring him in.''

Choosing the youngest over the eldest would go against the deeply ingrained attitudes and practices of a culture that favored the firstborn. Furthermore, relatively speaking, David was a mere lad. But the rugged, quiet shepherd's life had nurtured the embryo of a beautiful character.

Samuel knew by now that he must wait for God's signals. "And the Lord said, 'Arise, anoint him; for this is the one!' " (verse 12). The prophet obeyed, whatever consequences might result.

THE TRUE ANOINTING

The horn of anointing oil poured on his head symbolized the anointing that God alone could provide: "And the Spirit of the Lord came upon David from that day forward" (verse 13).

The Holy Spirit became his teacher, the source of his communion and inspiration. Some of his most inspiring songs and prayers originated during this period of his life, psalms that "in all coming ages [would] kindle love and faith in the hearts of God's people, bringing them nearer to the ever-loving heart of Him in whom all His creatures live." [1]

There on those lonely Judean hillsides, the education of the future ruler of Israel took place. The pasture became his classroom, and nature his textbook as he communed with the Author and Creator of all things.

And while the young man opened his heart and life more and more to the control of the Spirit, Saul closed his heart and mind, and "the Spirit of the Lord departed from Saul, and a distressing spirit from the Lord troubled him" (verse 14).

DAVID'S INTRODUCTION TO ROYALTY

Saul's battle with conscience and his resistance to the Spirit of God became so troubling that he became emotionally ill. Some of the royal attendants, recognizing the symptoms of illness, suggested soothing music as therapy.

Bethlehem was about 10 miles south of Saul's headquarters at Gibeah. [2] In God's providence, someone recommended David for his musical skill. But even more significantly, his spiritual qualities recommended him: "the Lord is with him" (verse 18). David's warmth and personable nature endeared him to the troubled king. "He loved him greatly, and he became his armorbearer" (verse 21). (The term *love* not only indicates personal affection but was also used in the ancient world for political loyalty.) The strains of David's harp [3] brought healing and relief to the king's fits of depression—at least for a while.

There in Saul's court, David received another important part of his education, a course in the "Responsibilities of Royalty" and another in "Pitfalls of Leadership to Avoid."

When Saul did not need David to minister to him, the young shepherd returned to Bethlehem to tend his father's flocks in the peace and quiet of the wilderness.

DAVID AND GOLIATH

Once again the Philistines had penetrated the foothills of western Judah. Saul mustered his forces, and the two armies faced each other across the Valley of Elah (or Terebinth, a type of tree), near Socoh, about 14 miles west of Bethlehem. The enemy taunted Saul with a different kind of threat as they challenged him to single combat. Combat by champion had been practiced by the Philistines in their Aegean homelands. Girded with his bronze helmet and armor, his javelin and huge spear at his side, Goliath terrified Saul and the men of Israel. Day after day for six weeks his defiant cry to fight echoed across the valley.

Israel's champion, the tall and formerly brave Saul, no longer depended on the Spirit of God to give him courage and to lead him against the enemy. The record does not mention the whereabouts of Jonathan, nor why Saul's commanding officer, Abner, did not come forward. Saul and his men seemed frozen with fear in the face of Goliath.

Meanwhile, both the suggestion of his father and the direction of an angel [4] led David to place his sheep in the care of another and travel to the battle front to take supplies and food to his three brothers in Saul's army. (Soldiers in the ancient world lived on what they could plunder in the field or what their families brought them. Saul's army had no supply corps to bring them food or equipment.)

As David approached his brothers, he heard Goliath hurling his insults at the Israelites. Quickly he surveyed the situation and sensed the depression and terror that pervaded Saul's men. Soon he learned of the king's offer to anyone with the courage to face the giant.

But neither bribe to fame prompted him to do, nor barb of insult from his jealous brother prevented him from doing, what he did. Stirred by the Holy Spirit, David found himself fired with a holy zeal for the honor of his God. "Who is this uncircumcised Philistine, that he should defy the armies of the living God?" (1 Sam. 17:26).

David's response was not naive, because he had repeatedly faced danger before. Encounters with predator animals in the wild had taught him self-preservation. His courage was not a presumptuous flaunting of his physical prowess, but rather sprang from a heart that had been in close communion with His Maker, one who knew by experience Yahweh's power to deliver and save.

His offer to Saul to take on the giant met with surprise: "You are but a youth" (verse 33). (The term *youth* or *lad* here is used more in the sense of servant or inexperienced rather than of age. David was of marriageable age, as we see when Saul soon offers him his daughter.) But David answered with assurance, "The Lord, who delivered me from the paw of the lion and . . . the bear, He will deliver me from the hand of this Philistine" (verse 37).

Wisely David rejected Saul's cumbersome armor as being totally unsuited to his inexperience. With staff in hand and his simple weapons—five smooth stones from the dry wadi that flowed through the valley—David approached Goliath. He was experienced with the sling, having often defended himself with one. Slings were the light artillery of the ancient world, and slingers formed an important part of Near Eastern armies. The ruins of besieged cities are full of sling stones. A sling stone was the size of a baseball, and a good slinger could hurl a stone at a velocity of up to 100 miles an hour. The recent *Intifadeh* of the occupied territories of Israel has demonstrated the deadly power of the ancient sling.

The giant's ridicule did not intimidate David. His answer fairly rang with confidence and triumph. "You come to me with a sword, with a spear, and with a javelin. But I come to you in the name of the Lord of hosts, the God of the armies of Israel, whom you have defied. This day the Lord will deliver you into my hand . . . that all the earth may know that there is a God in Israel'' (verses 45, 46).

The soldiers on both sides of the valley watched in nervous anticipation. Suddenly a stone whizzed through the air. With precision it struck Goliath a fatal blow to the head. The Philistines gasped in horror as their champion slumped to the ground. In great confusion they retreated from the victors. The elated Israelites rushed after their enemies, pursuing them to the vicinity of Gath and Ekron.

SAUL'S LOVE-HATE RELATIONSHIP WITH DAVID

Saul's question as to David's identity (verses 55-58) poses a real difficulty when compared to 1 Samuel 16:21, 22. One possibility is that the narrator has handled the subject topically, not necessarily in exact sequence. Or Saul may have felt threatened by David's success, as he did by that of his own son Jonathan. His question about David's identity could have been one of sarcasm and jealousy. Whatever the reason, one thing is for sure: from now on Saul would never need ask again, ''Who is this David?'' From that day on he became a fundamental part of the king's household. ''Saul . . . would not let him go home to his father's house anymore'' (1 Sam. 18:2).

The warmth and charm of David's personality soon endeared him to all who knew him, including the king's own family. His popularity among the people grew, too.

One day as the soldiers returned home from another Philistine encounter, the women sang David's praises: ''Saul has slain his thousands, and David his ten thousands'' (verse 7). It was too much for the already sullen king. The love-hate relationship toward David now intensified until it would consume Saul. From that day on he watched for an opportunity to kill David.

It came one day while David played his harp to soothe the distressed king. Twice Saul tried to pin him to the wall with his spear. And twice David narrowly escaped. The narrator tells us repeatedly that Saul feared David because the king sensed that the Lord was with him. And in his sick mind he knew that he had separated himself from God and from all hope.

Failing to destroy his competitor with the spear, Saul turned to intrigue and duplicity. Merab, the king's firstborn daughter, should have gone to David after his victory over Goliath. But her father had married her off to another. Now he offered Michal (who loved David) for a dowry of 100 dead Philistines. Surely it would be a convenient way to get rid of David. He couldn't possibly survive that many combats.

That failing, and David gradually gaining the respect and esteem of everyone, including the king's son Jonathan, Saul became more and more obsessed with destroying his supposed enemy. Jonathan reasoned with his father, appealing to him to recognize David's innocence. But to no avail. Sometimes for a brief period reason would prevail, and Saul would determine to spare David. But then rage and insane jealousy would again control him.

On one occasion Saul sent messengers to David's house to assassinate him. Michal, David's wife, aided him in escaping, and he fled to Samuel at Ramah. The two men went to Naioth, where a strange sequence of events took place. Saul, learning of David's whereabouts, sent men to seize him. Upon arriving, "the Spirit of God came upon the messengers of Saul, and they also prophesied" (1 Sam. 19:20). When Saul heard the unusual news, he sent a second delegation. Again the same thing happened. Then it happened a third time. Finally, he himself went to Samuel, only to have the supernatural phenomenon fall upon him. Was God trying one last time to reach his heart? Was Saul's strange response a substitute for genuine heart repentance and confession of sin? (see verse 24). Or was God using "the wrath of man" to praise Him by restraining evil? [5]

DAVID AND JONATHAN

If anyone had a right to be jealous of the popular David, it would have been Jonathan. As crown prince, he might have been the one to wish David out of the picture. But not so. David earned his respect and devotion. Early in their friendship they entered into a covenant, and Jonathan clothed David with his own royal robe and armor as a token of his loyalty to him. Evidently he already sensed that David would be the next king of Israel.

After the Naioth affair, David appealed to Jonathan to

intervene for him with his father. "But truly, as the Lord lives . . . there is but a step between me and death" (1 Sam. 20:3).

According to their agreement, Jonathan would convey Saul's response to David's absence at the new moon feast to him. (Anger would indicate the king's surveillance of his every move.) Unfortunately Saul made violent accusations against David (see verse 30), and in a fit of anger he tried to kill his own son.

Jonathan, now convinced of his father's hostile intent, grieved for his friend. He headed for their place of rendezvous to give him the sad news. Even the lad who picked up the signal arrows did not realize their meaning, but the two friends knew only too well. It would be one of the last times they would meet. Their parting words reaffirmed their devotion to each other, and their commitment even to each other's descendants. "May the Lord be between you and me, and between your descendants and my descendants, forever" (verse 42). David would never forget that promise to his beloved friend.

Once again, on their last visit in the wilderness of Ziph, the two friends confirmed their covenant. Jonathan boldly encouraged him, "You shall be king over Israel, and I shall be next to you" (1 Sam. 23:17). Some scholars have suggested that when Jonathan gave David his robe (1 Sam. 18:4) he was legally giving up and transferring his position as heir-apparent to the throne. Only unselfish love and mutual faith and trust in God could have bonded such a friendship. God had given David a brother-like friend to see him through difficult times and to help preserve his life.

The rare qualities exhibited by the two friends made for a unique friendship, one that has become a model for all time. "The soul of Jonathan was knit to the soul of David, and Jonathan loved him as his own soul" (verse 1). The Hebrew implies that their souls were "chained" together. Chained by a common bond of piety and love for God, by a sense of duty and loyalty to Him, their nation, and to each other. Jonathan willingly deferred the crown to his friend, while David magnanimously loved Jonathan in spite of his father's threats to his life.

Both men had a heart for God, committed first to Him and then to one another. Their friendship illustrates the best in human relationships. But even more significantly, it speaks to us of Him who sticks closer than a brother.

---

[1] *Patriarchs and Prophets*, p. 642.

[2] Excavations at Gibeah have revealed that Saul's palace was probably more like a rustic fortress. See D. F. Payne, *Kingdoms of Our Lord*, p. 28.

[3] Actually a lyre, according to H. F. Vos, *Commentary on Samuel*, pp. 61, 62.

[4] *Patriarchs and Prophets*, p. 645.

[5] *Ibid.*, p. 653.

Saul son Jonathan
and David were
like brothers
who loved one
and another dearly

CHAPTER

7

In the University of Adversity

G od had chosen a man of faith and large heart. A man who though easily moved by human emotions, was yet willing to be molded and shaped for great responsibilities. But before he received the crown, David must enter the University of Adversity for his doctoral program in leadership. At times he would excel, at other times the weakness and ragged edges of his character would stand shamefully exposed. But his hard-earned degree would prepare him to rule.

DAVID, A FUGITIVE

From the moment of David and Jonathan's sad farewell, David became a fugitive and an outlaw, the victim of insane jealousy. Staying in the king's court would jeopardize his own as well as Jonathan's safety. He dare not go to his home, for there he would put his family at risk. If he fled to his trusted friend and confidant, Samuel, Saul might take his revenge on the prophet. David had no safe retreat!

In his extremity he fled to the sanctuary at Nob, hoping that there he might find refuge. The location of Nob is unknown, but possibly may have been near Jerusalem. Some scholars believe that Mount Scopus may have been its site, others think it to have been the Mount of Olives. [1] The sanctuary had been moved there after the destruction of Shiloh by the Philistines. The ark, of course, was still with Abinadab at Kirjath-jearim.

David believed that God's presence resided in the sanctuary.

And he knew that his only safety was in God. Later, in his exile, unable to visit the sanctuary, he would write of his longing for its courts:

"How lovely is Your tabernacle, O Lord of hosts!
My soul longs, yes, even faints for the courts of the Lord;
My heart and my flesh cry out for the living God" (Ps. 84:1).

But even the sanctuary of God provided no safe retreat for the hunted fugitive. David planned to appeal to Ahimelech, the priest. But as he talked with him, he became painfully aware of the presence of Saul's chief herdsman, Doeg, the Edomite, who was apparently celebrating some religious occasion there. (Some have even suggested that Doeg may have been undergoing some penance ritual that would not make him feel the most kindly toward the priests there.) At the sight of him, fear and panic seized David. Under the pressure of the moment, he resorted to deception and lying to protect himself. Claiming to be on royal business, he asked for food for himself and his men, appealing to a Levitical provision that the priest might eat the bread after it was removed from the table of shewbread (Lev. 24:8, 9). What he forgot was, that in doing so, he now endangered the whole family of priests.

He who had so bravely met Goliath in the name of the Lord of hosts, now trembled at the thought of his enemies. The sword that he asked for from Ahimelech, that had previously symbolized his faith and confidence in God, now became a symbol of his faltering faith and attempt to take things into his own hands.

David was not the first nor the last man of God to fail after a success. Moses had struck the rock after he had seen God. Gideon had fallen into idolatry after the Lord had miraculously delivered him and his 300 men from the Midianites. Elijah would flee to a cave after his triumph on Mount Carmel.

One deception, one sin, too often paves the way for another. David now fled in terror to the Philistine king of Gath. He who had slain at least 100 Philistines now turned to them for help. When Achish recognized him, David again resorted to a ruse to protect himself. First Samuel 21:12-15 offers one of the saddest pictures of David on record. A man preparing for the dignity of royalty demeaned himself by pretending insanity.

Again David fled to the lonely, desolate Judean hills. The cave of Adullam, David's hiding place, is thought to be at the eastern end of the Valley of Elah, where earlier he had met Goliath. [2] He had become a guerrilla leader, collecting the politically and socially disadvantaged around him.

The word of David's exile brought family and friends to his side. His own once-jealous brothers now united with him for protection and support. (David probably wrote Psalm 133 during this time: "Behold, how good and how pleasant it is for brethren to dwell together in unity!" [verse 1].) [3] Others in debt or discontented with Saul's regime joined him. Soon David had rallied a force of 400. He now had a little kingdom of his own.

But Saul's madness threatened anyone connected with David. Fearing for his parent's safety, he arranged for them to find refuge with the king of Moab, perhaps because of his great-grandmother's Moabite ancestry. About this time the prophet Gad came to assist David, maybe sent there by Samuel.

But such support would also increase the odds of exposure. It was difficult to keep the existence of such a large group secret. If nothing else, they would have to have food supplies, and any purchases from merchants or raids on storehouses would give away their location. Saul soon heard of David's hiding place. When he saw that his efforts to destroy David were being thwarted, he accused his servants of conspiracy and reminded them that as members of the tribe of Benjamin they could not expect favors from the court of a tribesman of Judah, as David was.

Doeg, an opportunist, became informer and accuser. Perhaps he had a personal vendetta against the high priest, or he may have simply seen it as an opportunity to enhance his own standing with the king. For whatever reason, he now painted an exaggerated picture of what had actually taken place at Nob.

The infuriated king, who had spared the condemned king Agag, professing compassion, now decreed the execution of all who wore the linen ephod. Even the innocent inhabitants of Nob became victims of the murderous hands of Doeg and Saul's insane rage, fulfilling the prophecy made to Eli before his death (1 Sam. 2:31-33).

The sole survivor of the massacre, Abiathar, fled to David for protection. David now had both a prophet and a priest in his camp while Saul had neither. David's profile as Israel's next king loomed larger on the horizon. But his tests in the University of Adversity were far from finished.

Devastated and grieved by the news of the slaughter of the priests, David sadly confessed to Abiathar, "I have caused the death of all the persons of your father's house" (1 Sam. 22:22).

CHASING THE WRONG ENEMY

Saul, bent on crushing a conspiracy that didn't exist except in his own mind, failed to protect his domain from the real enemy. When the Philistines threatened and robbed the threshing floors of Keilah, a community not far from Adullam, David, as an astute military leader, felt it was time for action.

But before attacking the Philistines, he decided that he must first determine whether God approved. "Then David inquired of the Lord once again" (1 Sam. 23:4). Assured that God would give victory, David raided the enemy and saved the inhabitants of Keilah (verse 5).

The king, instead of rejoicing in the victory or recognizing it as an indication of David's loyalty, now gathered his forces against David and his men, and actually pursued them instead of the Philistines.

SONGS OF ADVERSITY

Fortunately for us, many of the "papers" David wrote while in the University of Adversity have been preserved. His prayers and songs of lament, [4] which comprise much of the hymnbook of ancient Israel, have blessed believers through the centuries, especially those who have suffered for their faith. Martin Luther commented that those being persecuted could best appreciate the Psalms.

Significantly, some of David's most inspiring declarations of faith and triumphant notes of praise occur in his prayers of lament. Even the record of David's occasional lapses into unbelief seems to emphasize the desperation and seriousness of his situation rather than merely dwell on his weaknesses.

While hiding in the cave of Adullam, David composed Psalm 57, "A Prayer in the Midst of Perils." He describes his persecutors in the following words:

"My soul is among lions; I lie among the sons of men
    Who are set on fire, whose teeth are spears and arrows,
    And their tongue a sharp sword" (verse 4).

In spite of his fear of those "who would swallow [him] up," he declares:

"In the shadow of Your wings I will make my refuge,
    Until these calamities have passed by" (verse 1).

The deeper his distress, the higher his exaltation of praise to God for mercy and deliverance:

"I will sing and give praise. Awake, my glory!
    Awake, lute and harp! I will awaken the dawn" (verses 7, 8).

According to its superscription, the thirty-fourth psalm grew out of David's embarrassing encounter with Achish at Gath:

"The angel of the Lord encamps all around those who fear Him,
    And delivers them" (verse 7).

"Many are the afflictions of the righteous,
    But the Lord delivers him out of them all" (verse 19).

"Oh, taste and see that the Lord is good;
    Blessed is the man who trusts in Him!
    Oh, fear the Lord, you His saints!
    There is no want to those who fear Him.
    The young lions lack and suffer hunger;
    But those who seek the Lord shall not
    lack any good thing" (verses 8-10).

When the Ziphites betrayed David's hiding place after the Keilah affair, he encouraged himself with the words of Psalm 11: "In the Lord I put my trust" (verse 1). He asked the question that many in trouble have asked: "If the foundations be destroyed, what can the righteous do?" (verse 3).

David's despair prompted him to ask other poignant questions:

"How long, O Lord? Will You forget me forever?

How long will You hide Your face from me? . . .
How long will my enemy be exalted over me?'' (Ps. 13:1, 2).

In Psalm 35 David pleaded for God's intervention against those "who hate[d] [him] without a cause" (verse 19). (Jesus quoted the words in John 15:25.)

Ironically, one of the most difficult courses David endured while attending the University of Adversity actually contributed most to his success as Israel's greatest king. His anguish and grief over the unjust exile and persecution that he suffered would make him forever more sensitive to the needs of the oppressed and downtrodden, a theme that appears frequently in the psalms attributed to him:

"Blessed is he who considers the poor;[5]
The Lord will deliver him in time of trouble" (Ps. 41:1).
"The Lord also will be a refuge for the oppressed,
A refuge in times of trouble" (Ps. 9:9; cf. Ps. 12:5; 62:10; 68:5, 6).

Psalm 63 recalled David's intense longing for God while hiding in the wilderness of Judah and rejoiced in His mercy:

"O God, You are my God; early will I seek You;
My soul thirsts for You; my flesh longs for You
In a dry and thirsty land where there is no water. . . .
Because Your lovingkindness is better than life,
My lips shall praise You.
Thus I will bless You while I live;
I will lift up my hands in Your name. . . .
And my mouth shall praise You with joyful lips" (verses 1, 3-5).

THE DEATH OF SAMUEL

Another severe blow to David's already beleaguered life was the death of the prophet Samuel, his spiritual mentor and confidant. Coming as it did after a very short-lived reconciliation with Saul, the future king now knew there was no safety for him anywhere. David mourned deeply Samuel's passing.

The nation had lost a great prophet and judge. His far-reaching influence, so much needed in that time of low spirituality, would be greatly missed. The prophet's death reminded the people of their terrible mistake in rejecting his leadership in exchange for a king. [5]

David realized that the loss of the prophet would mean one less restraint on the mad king. The political refugee now fled with his men to the wilderness of Paran in southern Judah. The desolate desert, inhabited by marauding tribes, would not provide a friendly reception to the exiles. Here, after a last brief visit from Jonathan, David composed Psalms 120 and 121:

"My help comes from the Lord, who made heaven and earth.

He will not allow your foot to be moved;

He who keeps you will not slumber" (Ps. 121:2, 3).

"The Lord shall preserve you from all evil;

He shall preserve your soul.

The Lord shall preserve your going out and your coming in

From this time forth, and even forevermore" (verses 7, 8).

A WOMAN'S GENTLE POWER

While in Paran, David and his men camped near the flocks of a wealthy herdsman, offering protection from marauders and beasts of prey in exchange for supplies. Scripture names the herdsman as Nabal, an adjective in Hebrew meaning foolish and senseless, especially in ethical and religious matters. Some scholars have suggested that the biblical writer deliberately suppressed the man's real name and simply called him by his nature.

David was now what we could call a desert warlord. When he needed provisions for his men, he sent messengers to request help from Nabal. Sheepshearing time was a festive occasion, similar perhaps to our Christmas season, a time of gift-giving and goodwill. [6]

According to Eastern custom, to turn down a plea for help at any time would be unacceptable. But to do so at sheepshearing time would be rude and hostile. The churlish Nabal pretended ignorance of David's identity. But even the servants seemed to know that David commanded respect and deserved better treatment than their master had given him.

They now hurried to Abigail, Nabal's beautiful and wise

wife, with the news that David had been so insulted and angered that all their lives were in danger. Perhaps it was not the first time that she had found it necessary to intervene in a crisis her husband had created. "For he is such a scoundrel that one cannot speak to him," the herdsmen declared of their own employer (1 Sam. 25:17).

At any rate, the servants seemed to sense that Abigail would know what to do. And they were right. She immediately went into action. After she quickly had provisions loaded on pack animals, she sent servants ahead to relay the news of her coming, and all of it without her husband's knowledge.

To hastily assemble "two hundred loaves of bread" and "five sheep already dressed" required more than spur-of-the-moment planning (especially without a freezer or premilled flour). She was a well-organized woman, always prepared for any emergency, a classic illustration of the virtuous woman of Proverbs 31.

Abigail was a woman of courage. Neither her ill-tempered spouse nor the angry David could intimidate her to silence when the occasion demanded bold action. Yet her real power was not so much her boldness as it was her humility and submissive spirit.

As she approached David, she "fell on her face . . . and bowed to the ground" (verse 23). But her first words to him are even more amazing. "On me, my lord, on me let this iniquity be!" (verse 24). She virtually took responsibility for Nabal's rash behavior. "Please forgive the trespass of your maidservant" (verse 28).

Such power, graced with womanly intuition, softened the heart of the offended soldier. Abigail tactfully reminded David that certainly the Lord would fight the battles of one destined to sit on the throne of Israel. That he need not take matters into his own hands by shedding blood to avenge himself. She appealed to him not to bring reproach on his good name by an act that would later bring him grief and remorse.

David responded with genuine courtesy and appreciation. "Blessed is your advice and blessed are you, because you have kept me this day from coming to bloodshed" (verse 33). The future king could take rebuke or advice in a spirit of humility. "Let the righteous smite me; it shall be a kindness. And let him reprove me; it shall be an excellent oil" (Ps. 141:5). One of the marks of a truly great man is that he willingly listens to advice, especially from the women in his life.

Gladly David received the gift Abigail had brought, and he sent her back in peace with the words, "See, I have heeded your voice and respected your person" (1 Sam. 25:35).

Abigail had a sense of her own worth and womanly dignity. She commanded the respect of others by exercising her power of influence—yes, even authority—when occasion demanded. But she did so with "a gentle and quiet spirit" that becomes "women professing godliness" (1 Peter 3:1-4; 1 Tim. 2:9, 10).

Nabal's wife is a model for all Christian women, especially those who find themselves living in less than ideal situations. Not even the most cantankerous person need rob us of the spirit of grace and sweetness that should characterize those who have the meek and lowly Lord Jesus dwelling within.

This beautiful woman had captivated David. Hearing of her husband's death, he immediately sent a proposal through some of his men: "David sent us to you, to ask you to become his wife" (1 Sam. 25:40).

Her response was equally enthusiastic. She "rose in haste . . . attended by five of her maidens . . . and became his wife" (verse 42).

David's education in the University of Adversity was not over yet, but his marriage to Abigail was a bright spot for which he could be thankful. Of all his wives (David acted within the accepted culture of his time), Abigail was probably the wisest of his choices. The influence of Nabal's wealthy widow would bless and encourage him as he continued his preparation for kingship, and enhance his life with her wisdom through both bad times and good.

---

[1] See *The SDA Bible Commentary,* vol. 2, p. 554.

[2] *Ibid.,* p. 559.

[3] See *Patriarchs and Prophets,* p. 658.

[4] A lament is a song of sorrow or distress that grows out of suffering or persecution. Laments generally consist of five parts: (a) a cry or appeal for help, (b) a statement of the problem or complaint,

(c) a petition or request to God, (d) the suppliant's vow to God, and (e) a chorus of praise to God.

[5] The word *poor* here means "helpless" or "powerless."

[6] See *Patriarchs and Prophets,* p. 663.

[7] *Ibid.,* p. 664.

8

Choices That Destroy

The contrasts between David and Saul were not so much that one man was good and the other bad. Both men had fine assets, and each had plenty of liabilities. Each had glaring inconsistencies of character, and each made his share of mistakes.

But most of all, both men made choices. David made many good ones, and some bad ones that cost him dearly. Saul made some good choices, but the wrong ones eventually destroyed him. The difference was that David willingly recognized his bad decisions and repented of them. Not only did Saul fail to stick by his good choices, but he refused to admit to his wrong ones, and persisted in them till they led to his demise.

Saul's decision to indulge himself in self-pity led to envy, jealousy, and an unjustified hatred that completely consumed him. Had Israel's first king let his better impulses control him, he would not have become a victim of his own emotional turmoil.

DAVID AND SAUL'S LAST ENCOUNTERS

Two of those better moments happened after surprise encounters with David. Shortly after the massacre of the priests and the Keilah affair (1 Sam. 23), David and his men fled to the wilderness of En Gedi, [1] where they hid in one of the caves common to that region.

Saul with his 3,000 men, hot on David's trail and headed for the beautiful oasis of En Gedi, also approached the caves where shepherds often sought shelter for their herds. Entering one of the caves to attend to his personal needs, he unwittingly placed himself at David's mercy. David's elated men suggested to their leader, "This is the day you've been waiting for!" But in his regard for sacred office, he replied, " 'The Lord forbid that I should do this thing to my master, the Lord's anointed.' . . . So David restrained his servants" (1 Sam. 24:6, 7). In fact, in his conscience "David's heart troubled him because he had cut Saul's robe" (verse 5).

In some matters his conscience seemed to have blind spots, however. (His acceptance of his world's tolerance of multiple marriage, especially for political purposes, for example.) Yet he had a sensitivity toward those things of God that he did understand. His generally high regard for human life stands out in a time and culture that often disregarded the value of the individual.

Had David entertained the same feelings that ruled Saul, he might have used the opportunity to get rid of his rival. But he chose instead to appeal to the king to see the incident as proof of his loyalty. "Know and see that there is neither evil nor rebellion in my hand, and I have not sinned against you. Yet you hunt my life to take it. Let the Lord judge between you and me, and let the Lord avenge me on you. But my hand shall not be against you" (verses 11, 12).

The king's affection for David (he addressed him as son— indeed, he was his son-in-law) and the emotion of the moment got the better of him. "Saul lifted up his voice and wept" (verse 16). Then he virtually admitted that David had proved his innocence: "You are more righteous than I . . . And you have shown this day how you have dealt well with me" (verses 17, 18).

Saul now asserted the truth he had been avoiding: "I know indeed that you shall surely be king, and that the kingdom of Israel shall be established in your hand" (verse 20). The two entered a covenant that David would show mercy to Saul's descendants, a promise that David would basically keep.

But Saul's good intentions, based on mere impulse, were short-lived. After Samuel's death, the king and his forces once more resumed their manhunt, now in the wilderness of Ziph. When David learned their location, he entered the camp by night with Abishai, his nephew and one of his outstanding warriors. They found Saul asleep with his sword by his side. Abishai wanted to strike at once. Again David spared the king's life. "The Lord forbid that I should stretch out my hand against the Lord's anointed" (1 Sam. 26:11).

Taking Saul's spear and jug of water, they quietly slipped out of the camp. Next morning David challenged Abner, Saul's commander in chief: "Why then have you not guarded your lord the king?" (verse 15). That taunt spurred in Abner bitter feelings that would dog David's ascent to the throne.

Saul, recognizing David's voice, addressed him as "son." Again David pleaded with the king to cease his pursuit: "Now therefore, do not let my blood fall to the earth. . . . For the king of Israel has come out to seek a flea, as when one hunts a partridge in the mountains" (verse 20). Like a dog scratching at fleas when he should be protecting his master's property, Saul had spent his energies hunting his supposed enemy.

DAVID FLEES TO THE PHILISTINES

Though Saul had responded to his plea with weak-willed assurance, David knew by now that he could not trust the king's intentions, no matter how sincere he might be at the moment Saul made his vow.

David, like a sand partridge in the wilderness (verse 20) that becomes too exhausted to run and falls victim to its pursuer, wondered how much longer he could endure the strain of his exile. Doubts filled his mind. How could he ever become king? And how could he escape Saul's malice?

As noted in the previous chapter, some of David's greatest songs of confidence originated in his hours of extremity and despair:

"From the end of the earth I will cry to You,
    When my heart is overwhelmed;
    Lead me to the rock that is higher than I.
    For you have been a shelter for me,
    And a strong tower from the enemy" (Ps. 61:2, 3).

Now everything overwhelmed him. Exhausted by his outlaw existence, his faith and patience faltering, David in desperation once again fled to the Philistines. But his reaction reflects that of many of us. How often, just when God is working out His will and purposes for us, we take things into our own hands. His ways are veiled in mystery, and because we cannot understand them, we panic and think God has forsaken us. We look to appearances instead of trusting in His promises. [2]

His flight to the Philistines is one of the darkest chapters in his life. He greatly jeopardized his people, for his defection would encourage the wily Philistines in their oppression of Israel. And he weakened his influence among his own people, who might now question his motives and his loyalty to God, and his fitness to reign over them. David had provided opportunity to bring reproach on himself and his nation.

Achish, flattered to think that David would seek refuge with him, provided protection and gave the town of Ziklag as a possession to him and his family, his army, and all their households. While living in Ziklag, David and his men frequently went on forays against the Amalekites and other neighboring peoples whom God had appointed to destruction. Saul had failed to accomplish the task, and David felt a responsibility to eliminate these peoples who were a constant threat to Israel. [3]

But David's decision to deceive Achish by leading him to believe that he had been out raiding Israelites added to the tangled web of circumstances David was weaving for himself, a web he would not easily escape. The moment of reckoning came when once again the Philistines declared war on Israel. David, in Oriental courtesy, volunteered his services. Achish, still trusting him implicitly, happily accepted his offer. But some of the Philistine lords, recognizing David's influence among the Israelites and understanding Hebrew loyalty, objected, and refused to allow him to join their forces in their invasion of the Judean hills. They feared he would defect to his own people and become a hazard to them.

The Philistine ruler apologized to David: "I know that you are as good in my sight as an angel [the term translated as "angel" in the Old Testament means "messenger"] of God" (1

Sam. 29:9). The Philistines considered David a good man, but the military leaders naturally considered it not wise to let him accompany their expedition. The words must have stabbed David's conscience as he thought of the duplicity he had practiced on his benefactor. But though his faith had faltered, God in His mercy delivered him from his impossible web, and spared him once more.

David knew that God had forgiven him and had not forsaken him in spite of his own lapse into doubt. Once more he could sing:

"You are my hiding place;
  You shall preserve me from trouble;
  You shall surround me with songs of deliverance" (Ps.
  32:7).

THE ZIKLAG AFFAIR

But David's troubles were not over yet. Though God had rescued him from the tangled web he had woven, some of the loose strands would still cause him great grief. While David and his men had reported for battle at Aphek, a roving band of Amalekites had attacked Ziklag, burning and sacking it and taking the women and children as captives.

Struck with horror and amazement, David and his men "wept, until they had no more power to weep" (1 Sam. 30:4). His soldiers, blaming him for the catastrophe and overwrought with grief and rage, were ready to stone him.

David's world had caved in on him. An exile hunted by a mad king, his wives and children in the hands of desert marauders—fated to death or slavery—and his own followers turned against him. With every earthly tendril now gone, he reached out and grasped the only secure thing left: "David strengthened himself in the Lord his God" (verse 6).

"Be merciful to me, O God, for man would swallow me up;
    . . .

  For there are many who fight against me, O Most High.
  Whenever I am afraid, I will trust in You. . . .
  I will not fear. What can flesh do to me?" (Ps. 56:1-4).
This time, instead of following impulse or passion, he

consulted the priest Abiathar to determine the Lord's will. The priest advised him to pursue the raiders, that he would recover all. David's calm thinking and quick action saved the day. His men rallied to him, and they set out to search through the Negev for their families.

Finding an Egyptian slave who had been left behind to die by his Amalekite master, they learned the location of the marauders' encampment. David and his men quickly attacked, and after an intense battle, recovered all of their families and possessions.

Some of David's men, weary and exhausted, had stayed by the supplies near the brook Besor. Now as they came to meet the victors, some "wicked and worthless men" wanted to deny them a share in the booty. Again David's sense of justice and fairness prevailed, and it became an ordinance in Israel that "as his part is who goes down to the battle, so shall his part be who stays by the supplies; they shall share alike" (1 Sam. 30:24).

In a conciliatory gesture, David sent gifts, some of the spoil, to the elders of Judah and to his friends (verses 26-31). Perhaps he realized intuitively that his long journey to kingship was nearly at an end.

SAUL'S LAST BAD CHOICE

If the news of the Philistine campaign against Israel had put David into a dilemma, it brought terror and panic to Saul. With the death of Samuel the prophet, his last ray of hope for a better life had faded. Because he had put to death the family of priests, he had nowhere to turn for help or guidance in the current crisis. "And when Saul inquired of the Lord, the Lord did not answer him, either by dreams or by Urim or by the prophets" (1 Sam. 28:6).

In desperation he tried a source he himself had previously outlawed. God had given, through Moses, specific instructions regarding spiritism and witchcraft. "And the person who turns after mediums and familiar spirits, to prostitute himself with them, I will set My face against that person and cut him off from his people" (Lev. 20:6). Knowing the evils of such practices, Saul had followed God's instructions and had all mediums and spiritists put to death.

Most ancient religions worshiped and attempted to communicate with the dead. Many tombs in Palestine had shafts leading up to the surface for the family to speak with the dead, and ritual meals at the gravesite with the deceased was common. The people believed that their dead ancestors were still part of the family and participated in its activities, sometimes causing mischief, other times warning of future events. Israelite religion rejected this, but such practices were a powerful temptation to God's people throughout the Old Testament period and even into New Testament times.

Now Saul's desperate mind made one last tragic choice, a decision that revealed the depths to which the once-noble king had fallen. Learning of a medium at En-dor, Saul disguised himself and sought her counsel: "Please conduct a seance for me, and bring up for me the one I shall name to you" (1 Sam. 28:8).

The woman objected on the grounds that her identity might become known to the king, threatening her safety. Saul reassured her and asked her to summon Samuel. Soon she realized that her client was none other than the king of Israel himself.

The conversation between Samuel and Saul has puzzled many Bible students. Did Samuel actually appear and talk with the Israelite king? Would God choose to communicate with the rejected king through a medium that He Himself had condemned, when He had refused to respond to him by all of the appropriate lines of communication, prophets, Urim and Thummim, etc.? The spirit that masqueraded as Samuel ascended "out of the earth" (it was a widespread belief in the ancient Near East that all the dead had their abode somewhere under the earth).

An evil spirit, assuming the prophet's role, delivered a message of doom and despair. His dire prediction of defeat and death struck terror to the already-fearful king.

Refusing at first to eat (he had fasted in preparation for consulting the medium), Saul finally acceded to the urgings of his servants and the medium, and ate what was probably his final meal. He who might have been feasting in a royal palace sits in the dingy abode and at the table of an outcast of Israel. The one who might have courageously led his forces to victory against the Philistines is about to march to an ignominious death. Such were the consequences of Saul's choices.

"So Saul died for his unfaithfulness which he had committed against the Lord, because he did not keep the word of the Lord, and also because he consulted a medium for guidance. But he did not inquire of the Lord; therefore He killed him, and turned the kingdom over to David" (1 Chron. 10:13, 14).

THE DEATH OF SAUL

The first book of Samuel ends with the sad account of Saul's death. "The men of Israel fled from before the Philistines, and fell slain on Mount Gilboa" (1 Sam. 31:1). How could they fight with courage when their leader had lost all hope? The prediction of the witch at En-dor had become a self-fulfilling prophecy for Saul.

The battle intensified. The archers fatally wounded the despondent king. Not wishing to die at the hand of the enemy, Saul begged his armorbearer to finish the job. (David had once been Saul's armorbearer.) When the man refused, the king threw himself on his sword, and took his own life. Thus came the inglorious end of what might have been a glorious career.

Saul's three sons, Jonathan, Abinadab, and Malchishua, and his armorbearer all died that day in battle. (The latter also took his own life after Saul's suicide.)

The Philistines, gloating over their victory, decapitated the fallen king and his sons and hung his armor in their temple and the bodies on the wall of Beth Shan. The men of Jabesh Gilead, remembering how Saul had rescued them years earlier, marched all night to retrieve the bodies and gave them an honorable burial. It was an act that David, at his anointing, would commend and reward (2 Sam. 2:2-6).

After David's return to Ziklag to rebuild and restore their homes, an Amalekite servant brought the tragic news of the death of Saul and his sons. Perhaps thinking he might find favor in David's eyes, he told a story that claimed responsibility for the king's death. But David's heart had no room for revenge or exultation over the death of the one who had hunted his life for so many months. Instead he was appalled that the man had lifted his hand against the Lord's anointed, something he himself would not do even under vastly different circumstances. With a sense of justice David commanded his immediate execution.

David's grief knew no bounds. His high regard for the fallen king, his great love for his friend Jonathan, and a sense of the terrible loss for the whole nation overwhelmed him with sorrow. He and his men "mourned and wept and fasted until evening for Saul and for Jonathan his son, for the people of the Lord and for the house of Israel, because they had fallen by the sword" (2 Sam. 1:12).

With deep emotion David wrote an elegy to the fallen king and princes, and instructed that it be taught to the children of Judah. It begins with a tribute to the slain, and a poetic dirge that the tragedy not be proclaimed in enemy territory:

"The beauty of Israel is slain on your high places!
How the mighty have fallen!
Tell it not in Gath, proclaim it not in the streets
of Ashkelon. . . .
Saul and Jonathan were beloved and pleasant in their lives,
And in their death they were not divided;
They were swifter than eagles, they were stronger than
lions.
O daughters of Israel, weep over Saul. . . .
How the mighty have fallen in the midst of the battle! (2
Sam. 1:19-27).

So ended the life of one who might have done great things for God. His own choices had destroyed him. The way was now open for David. Where would his decisions lead him?

---

[1] See *The SDA Bible Commentary,* vol. 2, p. 568, for a description of En Gedi.

[2] See *Patriarchs and Prophets,* p. 672.

[3] *Ibid.,* p. 673.

9

A King's Royal Resolves

DIFFICULT CHOICES

Israel's defeat at the hands of the Philistines dealt a severe blow to an already weakened and disheartened people. It may have seemed that all of Saul's efforts to overthrow the Philistine domination had been in vain. Who would pick up the pieces now that their leader was gone?

With Saul's death, David's exile ended and the way opened for him to assume the leadership of the nation. But between him and the throne lay a treacherous and sometimes bloody path and a series of difficult choices. David knew in his heart that God had destined him to be the next king of Israel. But he also realized that politically that path might be fraught with danger, even disaster. Would it be wise for him at this time to return to Judah? Would his people accept him after his stay in Philistine territory? Would they recognize God's intent that he be their next king? As he had done so often in the years of his exile, and as he would continue to do during most of his reign before acting upon some matter, "David inquired of the Lord" (2 Sam. 2:1).

"Teach me Your way, O Lord . . ." (Ps. 86:11).
"Teach me to do Your will, For You are my God; . . .
 Lead me in the land of uprightness" (Ps. 143:10).
"Cause me to know the way in which I should walk"
 (verse 8).
Acting on God's instruction, David returned to his homeland,

79

choosing to settle in the city of Hebron in the center of Judah. Hebron, also known as Mamre, the burial place of Abraham and his family, was the most important city in the territory of Judah at that time. David had spent much of his exile in that area, and knew that he would find a favorable reception.

And favorable it was! For as David and his men, their families, flocks, and herds entered the city, they received a royal welcome. Shortly after his arrival "the men of Judah came, and there they anointed David king over the house of Judah" (2 Sam. 2:4).

Had David attempted to rally the whole of Israel under his immediate control, he would have met with opposition. The 12 tribes did not have a strong sense of identity, as shown by how easily the monarchy broke up after the death of Solomon. Both David and Solomon were in a real sense not the kings of a single Israel, but rulers of a loose federation of individual tribes, which is why David had to be crowned more than once. Thus his choice to win Judah first showed skill in diplomacy. He now sent messengers to the men of Jabesh Gilead to honor them for their kindness to the memory of Saul, choosing to use the occasion to announce the fact that "the house of Judah has anointed me king over them" (verse 7). David's concern with honoring the slain Saul and his house helped to win greater support.

Meanwhile, the wily Abner, probably Saul's cousin, took it upon himself to declare Saul's only surviving son as king over the other tribes. Apparently he intended that the weak and vacillating Ishbosheth [1] would be a mere figurehead through whom he could exercise power.

The train of events that follow do not make for pleasant reading. But we must remember that in the time and culture in which Israel's monarchy began, the transfer of power from one dynasty to another frequently came about by revolution, insurrection, and bloodshed. David seemed not to be overly concerned about his rival in his remote capital at Mahanaim. [2]

But for his commander in chief, Joab, and Abner it was a different story. They arranged a dual between their men at Gibeon that resulted in bloodshed and loss of life. As Abner fled from the encounter, Asahel, the fleet-footed brother of Joab, pursued him hotly. Ignoring Abner's warnings to turn aside, the young man died from the spear of the pursued. Shortly afterward, Joab and Abner called a truce, but the conflict between them was far from over: "Now there was a long war between the house of Saul and the house of David. But David grew stronger and stronger, and the house of Saul grew weaker and weaker" (2 Sam. 3:1). Abner despised the weak puppet king he had set up, and when accused of a misdeed, threatened to change his loyalties and that of the tribes to Judah's new king. David took advantage of the opportunity to recall Michal, his wife and Saul's daughter, whom the dead king had previously given to another man.

The picture of Michal's husband, Paltiel, following her with weeping and pleading (see verse 16) is a poignant one, incomprehensible to our Western and Christian way of thinking. But it must be understood, if it cannot be justified, in its political setting. By regaining Michal, David further solidified his claim on the throne. As Saul's daughter, Michal could be seen as being able to pass on to her husband an inherited claim to Israel's kingship. Such attempts to tie up the loose ends of succession appear behind a number of the stories in the books of Samuel, Kings, and Chronicles. (For example, when Absalom went in to David's concubines after his father had fled Jerusalem [2 Sam. 16:20-23], it was to strengthen his claim on the throne.)

Abner's defection to David could mean a landslide in favor of David. But Joab, returning to Hebron and learning of Abner's proposal, felt threatened in his position, and used the occasion to seek personal revenge on Abner, who had slain his brother Asahel (2 Sam. 3:24-27). David's comment to some of his inner circle after the brutal murder of Abner revealed his frustration: "I am weak today, . . . and these men, the sons of Zeruiah, are too harsh for me" (verse 39).

Though David felt he could not provide justice in this case because of a number of complicated factors, including the power and position of his nephews, Joab and Abishai, he made it clear that he abhorred the deed, and declared a period of mourning for the slain leader of Saul's army. He himself followed the bier at a state funeral. "Do you not know that a prince and a great man has fallen this day in Israel?'' (verse 38). Impressed by the king's genuine grief and his declaration that he had no part in the assassination, ''the people took note of it, and it pleased them'' (verse 36).

The news of Abner's death brought fear to Ishbosheth, who realized that he had no actual power of his own. Soon afterward two of his servants assassinated him. Again David's sense of justice and his magnanimous spirit toward the house of Saul caused him to execute those who had perpetrated the crime (see 2 Sam. 4:9-12).

DAVID ANOINTED KING OVER ISRAEL

His spirit of fairness and equity, and his abilities as a leader had won the hearts of Israel. He had given evidence that concern for his people, not personal ambition, motivated him in his decisions.

David demonstrated the principle of servant-leadership that his Son, the Messiah, would so beautifully exemplify and teach a thousand years later: ''Whoever desires to be great among you, let him be your servant. . . . Just as the Son of Man did not come to be served, but to serve'' (Matt. 20:26-28).

The leaders of the various tribes now journeyed to Hebron to declare their pledge of loyalty: ''Indeed we are your bone and your flesh. . . . The Lord said to you, 'You shall shepherd My people Israel, and be ruler over Israel.' So all the elders of Israel came to the king at Hebron, and King David made a covenant with them . . . before the Lord'' (2 Sam. 5:1-3).

David's ascendance to the throne of the whole nation came about—especially when compared to other changes of government in the ancient Near East—in a quiet, dignified revolution, without excessive force or great bloodshed.

A large segment of the population gathered in the vicinity of Hebron for the coronation of their king. [3] It must have been impressive, with David in royal regalia, the priests and Levites in their sacred attire, and the officers and soldiers with glittering spears and helmets. [4] The coronation of King David at Hebron was the third time the sacred oil had been placed on his brow. Samuel had anointed him in a prophetic gesture, and the people of Judah had anointed him seven years earlier. Now with the scepter placed in his hand, the diadem on his brow, David became king of all Israel by divine appointment. [5]

DAVID CHOOSES A NEW CAPITAL

One of David's first priorities as Israel's new king was to select a capital that would be more centrally located and acceptable to all the tribes. Saul had come from the small tribe of Benjamin, but Judah, which had produced the new king, would be more of a political threat to the other tribes, especially to the influential northern tribe of Ephraim. Now that the 12 tribes had crowned a common king, David decided to do everything he could to bond that unity. He wanted a neutral site for Israel's new capital, one that would not carry an obligation to any tribe.

About 20 miles north of Hebron, and about five miles from Bethlehem, David's birthplace, lay the fortress of Jebus. The Israelites had never conquered the important stronghold, even in Joshua's time. It was still inhabited by a Canaanite people known as Jebusites. They boasted that their city, surrounded by hills and valleys, was so impregnable that even the blind and lame could defend it (verse 6).

The fortress lay on a narrow ridge with deep wadi valleys on either side of it. All north-south traffic through Palestine would need either to go by way of this ridge or confront incredibly difficult travel through the valleys. [6]

Jerusalem had been a strategic city for centuries. Early Egyptian records refer to the city as "Urushalim." Abraham paid tithe to Melchizedek, king of Salem. And as already mentioned, the Jebusites had occupied the city at least since the days of Joshua and prided themselves on their well-protected garrison.

Two hills or ridges on the site, known as Ophel and Zion, surrounded by deep natural valleys, made the city easily defensible. From Ophel on the east is an almost vertical slope down to the Kidron Valley, which provides a better defense than man could build. [7]

It is not difficult to understand, then, why David wanted the strategic village as his capital. In addition, since the site had never belonged to any Israelite tribe, it would have no obligations to anyone except its conqueror David. He had herded his sheep on the hillsides of Bethlehem, and probably with boyish curiosity had roamed the surrounding area. Doubtless he knew that Jebus had its own natural water supply flowing from the spring Gihon. The Jebusites had cut a water shaft from the Gihon into a reservoir some 60 feet away, which in turn connected to a 40-foot vertical shaft leading up to a kind of stairway or ramp, giving the city a natural and accessible water supply. [8]

Scholars believe that David now challenged his men with the promise that whoever would be first to enter the city by way of the water shaft should be chief of his armed forces (verse 8; cf. 1 Chron. 11:6). Joab accomplished the difficult feat, and confirmed his place as commander in chief of David's forces. [9]

By eliminating the natural barrier between Judah and the other tribes caused by the hostile Jebusite fortress, David brought the nation into greater unity geographically, and he had chosen a location on the border between Judah and Benjamin that would politically satisfy all the tribes.

"So David dwelt in the stronghold, and called it the City of David" (2 Sam. 5:9). Choosing the eastern hill, now known as Ophel, David proceeded to establish his capital, rebuilding the wall, and calling his city Mount Zion. [10] There he would preside for the remainder of his 40-year reign.

VICTORY OVER ENEMIES

"So David went on and became great, and the Lord God of hosts was with him" (verse 10). But the Philistine threat had not ceased. Sensing Israel's strength under a new king, they now camped in the Valley of Rephaim (probably the Valley of Hinnom) on the very outskirts of David's city. [11] Immediately he turned to the Lord for guidance as to his course of action. Following God's instructions carefully, his men advanced, accompanied by unseen hosts, and drove the enemy into retreat (verses 23-25). David knew that "no king is saved by the multitude of an army" (Ps. 33:16) and that the Lord of Hosts was his only security in battling his enemies.

"Some trust in chariots, and some in horses;
But we will remember the name of the Lord our God"
(Ps. 20:7).

Sometime later David again "attacked the Philistines and

subdued them'' (2 Sam. 8:1), making them tributary to him. Some of them even joined his personal army. For the major part of his reign the Philistines no longer seemed to offer a significant threat to Israel.

David continued to assert his power over Israel's enemies, receiving tribute from many of them. But he treated even his enemies humanely whenever possible. Nahash, the Ammonite king, had shown kindness to him while he was a fugitive from Saul. Now upon his death, David sent a message of sympathy to his son. But the Ammonites, who had threatened the people of Jabesh Gilead with putting out their eyes (in the days of Saul), now judged David's gesture by their own motives. They treated David's ambassadors (2 Sam. 10:4) with humiliating insult and contempt. Then as now such an indignity done to the ambassadors of another nation demanded prompt retaliation. [12]

"When the people of Ammon saw that they had made themselves repulsive to David, . . . [they] hired the Syrians" (verse 6) to fight against Israel. As Joab rallied his men, he realized that the Ammonites besieged his forces from both front and behind (verse 9). Choosing some of Israel's most skilled soldiers, he "put them in battle array" against the Syrians. "The rest of the people he put under the command of Abishai his brother" (verse 10) to defend against the Ammonites. Then Joab challenged his men to "be of good courage, and let us be strong for our people and for the cities of our God" (verse 12).

DAVID'S RIGHTEOUS REIGN

While God's purpose for Israel included judgment on the wicked nations whose cup of iniquity had filled to the brim, His greater desire was to reveal His character to the human family. He would demonstrate the operations of His kingdom through an earthly monarchy built on the principles of righteousness.

David had virtually completed the work begun by Joshua, that of subduing Israel's enemies and of establishing a kingdom that would resound the praises of the Great King and lead the people of other nations to join them in worshiping Him.

"So David reigned over all Israel; and David administered judgment and justice to all his people" (2 Sam. 8:15).

He had made a covenant with both his friend Jonathan and Saul to remember their posterity with kindness. He now sought out any living descendant of the former royal family. Learning of the handicapped son of Jonathan, who had become lame as a result of an accident when a nurse fled with him from the murderers of Ishbosheth (2 Sam. 4:4), David summoned him. The king assured Mephibosheth that his rightful possession would be restored to him, and that he would find favor in David's eyes as long as he lived. Furthermore, he would live in Jerusalem and eat at the king's table (2 Sam. 9:7).

Early in his reign David had made a commitment to order his household and his kingdom by the principles of righteousness. He sang of his resolves in Psalm 101:

"I will behave wisely in a perfect way . . .
I will walk within my house with a perfect heart.
I will set nothing wicked before my eyes;
I hate the work of those who fall away; . . .
A perverse heart shall depart from me;
I will not know wickedness. . . .
He who works deceit shall not dwell within my house;
He who tells lies shall not continue in my presence"
(verses 2-7).

Had David always applied such principles in his personal life and family dealings, how different his future history might have been. What heartache and woe might he have averted had he continued to live by such high ideals, especially in his family relationships.

While David's reign was not perfect, he would come closer to demonstrating the ideal than any other king. It was Israel's golden age, its finest hour. David's choices so far had brought blessing and honor to himself, his people, and most important, to his God.

Late in his reign, when David knew the kingship would soon pass to his son, he composed Psalm 72 as a charter for an ideal reign, a charter that would not be fulfilled until his Son, the Messiah, would come to earth to set up His kingdom in the hearts and lives of men and women:

"Give the king Your judgments, O God,

And Your righteousness to the king's Son.
He will judge Your people with righteousness,
And Your poor with justice" (verses 1, 2).
"He will save the children of the needy,
And will break in pieces the oppressor" (verse 4).
"He shall come down like rain upon the mown grass,
Like showers that water the earth" (verse 6).
"He shall have dominion also from sea to sea,
And from the River to the ends of the earth" (verse 8).
"His name shall endure forever;
His name shall continue as long as the sun.
And men shall be blessed in Him;
All nations shall call Him blessed" (verse 17).

---

[1] The name is actually Ishbaal. Some scholars see in it a hint that his mother may have been a Canaanite, the result of a political marriage.

[2] Mahanaim, located on the eastern side of the Jordan, offered protection from David and the Philistines. (See *Patriarchs and Prophets*, p. 699.)

[3] See *Patriarchs and Prophets*, p. 701.

[4] *Ibid.*, p. 702.

[5] *Ibid.*

[6] For a geographical description of Jerusalem, see Hershel Shanks, *The City of David* (Washington, D.C.: Biblical Archaeology Society, 1973), pp. 15, 16.

[7] *Ibid.*, p. 17.

[8] See *The SDA Bible Commentary*, vol. 2, p. 620.

[9] Hershel Shanks spends considerable time showing that it was indeed possible, though difficult, to have accomplished this feat. See *City of David*, pp. 31-37.

[10] For years scholars believed that David's Mount Zion was located on the west side. More recent excavations have shown that David's city occupied the eastern hill. See *The SDA Bible Dictionary*, p. 1182.

[11] See *The SDA Bible Commentary*, vol. 2, p. 622.

[12] See *Patriarchs and Prophets*, pp. 714, 715.

10

When God Says No

DAVID DECIDES TO MOVE THE ARK

David had established his throne in Jerusalem. He had won the devotion and allegiance of his own people. And his military feats had earned the fear and respect of the surrounding nations. Now he would seek the honor and glory of God's name by bending his energies to finding a home for the sacred ark in his new capital.

"So David knew that the Lord had established him as king over Israel, and that He had exalted His kingdom for His people Israel's sake" (2 Sam. 5:12).

Moses had given repeated instructions that God Himself would designate Israel's place of worship: "You shall seek the place where the Lord your God chooses . . . to put His name for His habitation; and there you shall go" (Deut. 12:5; see also Deut. 16:2; 26:2; 31:11).

Since the destruction of Shiloh [1] the sanctuary had resided at Gibeon (see 1 Chron. 16:39; 2 Chron. 1:3). But the very heart and center of Israel's worship, the sacred ark, was not there. For some 20 years, since the return of the ark from the Philistines, Abinadab, a Levite, had taken care of it at Kirjath-jearim.

Because David understood God's intention that Israel be a miniature replica of the true divine monarchy, he cherished a plan to make the capital of his kingdom the center of Israel's worship and home of the sacred ark. As the first phase of his plan he would bring the neglected ark to Jerusalem. Having accomplished that, he would turn his attention to building a fitting temple to house it.

David now called for a large representation of the leading men of Israel to participate in what he purposed to be a most impressive occasion of religious ceremony and pageantry. The king himself led the procession, accompanied by instrumental and choral music (2 Sam. 6:1-5).

TRAGEDY STRIKES

When they arrived at the house of Abinadab, David had the ark placed on a new cart, and Uzzah and Ahio, ''sons'' (probably grandsons) of Abinadab drove it on its way. Suddenly, amid the rejoicing and celebration, there fell a deadly silence. The people stood frozen in terror (see verses 6, 7).

Royal guards entered the crowd to carry away the body of a dead man. As quietly as possible, officials advised the celebrants to return to their homes. Fear and questioning hovered over the multitude as they made their way from the site of the tragedy.

The terrible details passed in whispered tones from one person to another. When the oxen stumbled, perhaps stooping to snatch a bit of hay or grain in Nachon's threshing floor, the cart carrying the sacred chest had begun to sway. Uzzah, reaching out to steady the ark, had been stricken as if by lightning. How could it be other than a judgment of God?

David, angered that the happy occasion should be marred by such a severe judgment (verse 8), called a halt to the whole ceremony, naming the place Perez Uzzah (literally, ''an outburst against Uzzah''). He had the ark quickly taken to the nearest safe place, the house of Obed-Edom the Gittite. One tradition suggests he may have been a member of the Levite family assigned to transport the ark (cf. 2 Sam. 6:7-10). [2] Or he could have been a Philistine, one of those who had joined David's service beginning with his sojourns in Gath and Ziklag. (Textual scholars feel that his name indicates he was a citizen of the Philistine city of Gath, and Obed-Edom itself means a worshiper of the god Edom.) If the latter, could his selection have been an allusion to the fact that the Philistines treated the ark with greater respect after their capture of it years earlier than God's own people had?

"David was afraid of the Lord that day; and he said, 'How can the ark of the Lord come to me?' " (verse 9). His hopes for housing the ark in his city had been dashed and his faith shaken.

But his relationship to his God could withstand even his momentary anger and fear. When the emotion of the occasion had subsided, David began to ask some questions: Would God have acted with such severity without cause? Had the people carefully followed divine instructions in their plans to transport the sacred chest? Or had Uzzah knowingly or carelessly violated a sacred command when he touched the sacred chest? [3] David searched the law of Moses to determine what had gone wrong and how to correct the mistakes. He watched intently to see what would now happen to the house of Obed-Edom while the ark remained in his home.

DAVID MOVES THE ARK TO JERUSALEM

Seeing that God blessed the house of Obed-Edom (verse 11), David determined to try once again to bring the ark to Jerusalem, this time carefully following Levitical instructions (see 1 Chron. 15:2; cf. Num. 4:5, 6, 15; 7:9). No Philistine oxcart now, but the appointed priests carrying it with staves on their shoulders.

David had learned by disappointment something that Saul had failed to grasp—that to obey is better than sacrifice. From the experience he wrote Psalm 24. The first part of the psalm asks the question: "Who may ascend into the hill of the Lord? Or . . . stand in His holy place?" (verse 3).

The answer is simple and clear:

"He who has clean hands and a pure heart,

   Who has not lifted up his soul to an idol,

   Nor sworn deceitfully" (verse 4; cf. Ps. 15).

"And so it was, . . . God helped the Levites who bore the ark of the covenant" (1 Chron. 15:26). Led by their king, the elders of Israel, military officers, and "all Israel" (verses 25, 28) make their way from the house of Obed-Edom to Jerusalem with rejoicing and sacred celebration.

The triumphal procession advances with the sound of praise and musical instruments, some of which David had designed himself. A large choir swells its voices to announce the approach of the ark, the dwelling place of their true King:

"Lift up your heads, O ye gates;
  And be lifted up, you everlasting doors!
  And the King of glory shall come in" (Ps. 24:7).
Back comes the query:
"Who is this King of glory?"
And from another antiphonal choir the joyous response:
"The Lord strong and mighty,
  The Lord mighty in battle" (verse 8).

The chorus is repeated, and the whole multitude responds. It is a chorus that will be echoed at the final great entrance of the King of kings and Lord of lords to rule the earth with righteousness. (See Rev. 5:13; 19:13-16.)

David had fulfilled the first phase of his vow. He sings of it in Psalm 132:

"Surely I will not go into the chamber of my house,
  Or go up to the comfort of my bed;
  I will not give sleep to my eyes
  Or slumber to my eyelids,
  Until I find a place for the Lord,
  A dwelling place for the Mighty God of Jacob"
    (verses 3-5).
"Arise, O Lord, to Your resting place,
  You and the ark of Your strength.
  Let Your priests be clothed with righteousness,
  And let Your saints shout for joy" (verses 8, 9).

A DISCORDANT NOTE

Only one discordant note marred the occasion. David's wife, Michal, watching from the palace window, saw him lay aside his royal robes for the plain dress of the common priests, and join with the people in sacred dance and song to celebrate the happy occasion. [4] Bitter feelings of resentment and hatred, probably rankling within her heart since Abner had brought her back to her rightful husband, now stirred within her.

"Then David returned to bless his household. And Michal the daughter of Saul came out to meet [him]" (2 Sam. 6:20). A torrent of sarcasm and false accusations poured forth from her lips. David's rebuke to her implies that she had despised not just her husband but the sacred service being celebrated (verses 21, 22).

None of David's wives seem to have been referred to as queen. Perhaps Michal may have coveted the title. No doubt a beautiful and stately woman, she longed for the power and glory that had so elusively evaded her father, and now seemed beyond her reach as David's wife. She despised him for his humility and self-effacing love for God that condemned her own pride.

The proud and arrogant cannot tolerate a spirit of meekness and humility that lays bare their own spiritual deformity and nakedness. Jesus emphasized this when He said: "Blessed are the meek. . . . Blessed are those who are persecuted for righteousness' sake" (Matt. 5:5-10). Paul understood it when he declared that "all who desire to live godly in Christ Jesus will suffer persecution" (2 Tim. 3:12). Michal had let her disappointment in life fester until it turned into persecuting anger.

DAVID'S KING

The stage was now set for a stronger, more united Israel that through its unique monarchy would demonstrate the principles of God's kingdom. The Lord had chosen a king who understood that his earthly kingship reflected but dimly the glory of the true King. David's awareness of this fact appears throughout his psalms:

"The Lord is King forever and ever" (Ps. 10:16).
"The Lord sits as King forever" (Ps. 29:10).
"The Lord's throne is in heaven" (Ps. 11:4).

He saw himself as a servant-king who would shepherd his flock with the love and concern of the great King above.

"He also chose David His servant,
And took him from the sheepfolds; . . .
To shepherd Jacob His people, and Israel His inheritance.
So he shepherded them according to the integrity of his heart,
And guided them by the skillfulness of his hands"
(Ps. 78:70-72).

"Give ear, O Shepherd of Israel,
  You who lead Joseph like a flock;
  You who dwell between the cherubim, shine forth!"
    (Ps. 80:1).
He declared his own capital as the "city of the great King"
(Ps. 48:2).
"Great is the Lord, and greatly to be praised
  In the city of our God, in His holy mountain.
  Beautiful in elevation, the joy of the whole earth,
  Is Mount Zion, . . . The city of the great King"
    (verses 1, 2).
Psalm 2 may have been written for his own coronation, but
reflects prophetically the Kingship of the coming Messiah:
"Yet I have set My King
  On My holy hill of Zion. . . .
  The Lord has said to Me,
  'You are My Son, today I have begotten You.
  Ask of Me, and I will give You
  The nations for Your inheritance,
  And the ends of the earth for Your possession' "
    (verses 6-8; cf. Acts 4:23-30).
To his divine King David owed his full and total allegiance:
"Give heed to the voice of my cry,
  My King and my God" (Ps. 5:2).
"You are my King, O God" (Ps. 44:4).
"For the Lord Most High is awesome;
  He is a great King over all the earth" (Ps. 47:2).
"The Lord shall reign forever—
  Your God, O Zion, to all generations" (Ps. 146:10).
Such a great King deserved a house befitting His glory. To
that end David would now turn his attention.

TO BUILD A HOUSE FOR GOD

David's desire to erect a temple for God grew into a dream,
and his dream became a passion. How could he, as Yahweh's
servant-king, reside in a royal residence while the ark, symbol of
God's very presence, dwelt in a tent? His artistic mind envisioned
a magnificent temple, richer than any king's palace, where the

sacred ark might have a permanent home.

But before attempting to build such a house for God, he sought divine guidance. Calling the court prophet, Nathan, he outlined his plans. "See now, I dwell in a house of cedar, but the ark of God dwells inside tent curtains" (2 Sam. 7:2).

Impressed with the king's plans, Nathan responded with enthusiasm: "Go, do all that is in your heart, for the Lord is with you" (verse 3). But that same night the word of the Lord came to the prophet with a startling answer to the king's request. "No, David, you must not build a house for Me. All these years I've dwelt in a tent, moved about in the wilderness, and I've never asked anyone to build me a house of cedar" (see verses 6, 7). "I've appointed you to shepherd my people Israel. I've cut off your enemies and made you a great name among the nations but the work of building a house for Me must be for another, one whose hands have not been stained by blood" (verses 8, 9, 12, 13).

With what keen disappointment and pain David must have listened to the prophet's message. He might have become angry or impatient or argued with God—"Look how qualified I am to do this job, why are You putting me off?" Or he might have become bitter: "If You won't let me do what I want to do, I'll not do anything." But David had long since learned to trust his King even when the answer was no! His response reveals a spirit of submission to the divine will: "Who am I, O Lord God? And what is my house, that You have brought me this far? . . . Now what more can David say to You? For You, Lord God, know Your servant. For Your word's sake, and according to Your own heart, You have done all these great things, to make Your servant know them" (verses 18-21). And what was the key to his submission to God's will? David sensed the Lord's greatness and his own relationship of creature to Creator: "Therefore You are great, O Lord God. For there is none like You, nor is there any God besides You" (verse 22).

God then gave to David, His undershepherd, a wonderful promise concerning His people: "Moreover I will appoint a place for My people Israel, and will plant them, that they may dwell in a place of their own and move no more; nor shall the sons of wickedness oppress them anymore, as previously'' (verse 10).

Had Israel remained in covenant relation to their God, obeying His commands and precepts—had their kings maintained the servant-king relationship that David had modeled—Israel indeed would have been ''planted'' securely in their land ''to move no more.'' They need not have gone into captivity repeatedly and felt the constant oppression of enemies who wished to destroy them.

God had great plans for Israel. Plans that never fully materialized because of their unbelief, but will be fulfilled to His modern Israel (Gal. 3:27-29) when He finally brings us to the Promised Land (Rev. 21:1-5). There we will dwell in a place of our own and wander no more (a promise that can best be appreciated by those who have moved about all their lives, never living or becoming established in one place for more than a few short years).

GOD WILL BUILD A HOUSE FOR DAVID

And God had plans for the king, plans that would reach beyond him and his day, even into all eternity.

Though God had said no to David, He also said yes! The Lord through Nathan added, ''Also the Lord tells you that He will make you a house. When your days are fulfilled and you rest with your fathers, I will set up your seed after you, . . . and I will establish his kingdom. . . . And your house and your kingdom shall be established forever before you. Your throne shall be established forever'' (1 Sam. 7:11-16).

The play on words used here by the prophet is significant. God would build a house—a dynasty for David, and the work of building a house for God must be left to his house in the person of his son.

The Hebrew words used for *build* and *establish* appear frequently in Scripture. They portray God in His work of creation (Gen. 2:22) and in His acts of salvation (Ps. 69:35). God builds and plants His people (as noted in 2 Sam. 7:10; cf. Jer. 31:4; 24:6; 33:7), and He builds Zion, His dwelling place among His people (Ps. 102:16; Isa. 14:32). Here, as elsewhere, He builds or establishes a family or dynasty. ''Unless the Lord builds the house, they labor in vain who build it'' (Ps. 127:1).

The Lord's promise to David to establish an endless dynasty for him must be understood as a Messianic prophecy. The line of David's descendants continued to reign as long as the monarchy of Judah existed. With the Babylonian captivity came an end to the earthly Davidic dynasty. Yet God's promise repeatedly declared that the throne of his kingdom would be "established forever."

The early apostles based their preaching to their fellow Jews on such promises: ''He raised up for them David as king. . . . From this man's seed, according to the promise, God raised up for Israel a Savior—Jesus'' (Acts 13:22, 23; see also Acts 2:25-36). To this Son of David, God says, ''I will give you the sure mercies of David'' (Acts 13:34).

The sure mercies of David, based on the covenant promise, provide the theme of Psalm 89:

> ''I have made a covenant with My chosen,
> I have sworn to My servant David:
> 'Your seed I will establish forever,
> And build up your throne to all generations' '' (verses 3, 4).

> ''But My faithfulness and My mercy shall be with him,
> And in My name his horn shall be exalted.
> Also I will set his hand over the sea,
> And his right hand over the rivers.
> He shall cry to Me, 'You are my Father,
> My God, and the rock of my salvation.'
> Also I will make him My firstborn,
> The highest of the kings of the earth.
> My mercy I will keep for him forever,
> And My covenant shall stand firm with him.
> His seed also I will make to endure forever,
> And his throne as the days of heaven'' (verses 24-29).

> ''My covenant I will not break,
> Nor alter the word that has gone out of My lips.
> Once I have sworn by My holiness;
> I will not lie to David:
> His seed shall endure forever'' (verses 34, 35).

The greatest honor that the God of heaven could confer on

mortal man—to be the progenitor of the Messiah—He had promised to David. Because David had chosen God as his king-supreme, the Lord had granted him a house that would last forever.

His seed, the Saviour of the world, reigns now in the hearts and lives of His followers. One day soon He will come as Lord of lords and King of kings, and His throne, the throne of David, will rule the universe throughout the ceaseless ages of eternity.

---

[1] *The SDA Bible Dictionary,* p. 1003, suggests that archaeological evidence supports the assumption that the Philistines destroyed Shiloh at the battle of Aphek (1 Sam. 4:1-11) even though the record does not specifically state so.

[2] See *The SDA Bible Commentary,* vol. 2, p. 626.

[3] See *Patriarchs and Prophets,* pp. 705, 706.

[4] *Ibid.,* pp. 708, 711.

11

When Temptation Lurks

THE REST OF THE STORY

News commentator Paul Harvey frequently tells a little-known incident or background story about some well-known person or event, and closes with "And now you know the rest of the story."

The tragic incident in 2 Samuel 11, much as we might wish the author had omitted it (as it is in both Kings and Chronicles), is really the "rest of the story" of David's otherwise glorious reign. How could one whom God had so highly honored stoop so low? How could a man with a deep abiding faith, born of years of suffering and adversity, whose mind enjoyed exalted insights to the greatness and majesty of his God, become a victim of his own passion and weakness?

That question has haunted believers for centuries, and emboldened the wicked in their rebellion against God and His righteous ways. "See, not even a mighty individual like David had the strength to live up to God's high ideals and obey His holy commands!"

In a very real sense, however, the story of David's fall is that of the entire human family. In his tragic choice we may see a replay of the Fall of the human race in the Garden of Eden, when one moment's indulgence opened the floodgates of woe, misery, and degradation on a whole planet.

David's experience painfully reflects that of each one of us.

Our struggle with the power of temptation, our weakness and vulnerability to sin, our remorse when our bad choices make us victims of our own evil natures.

Yet, in the "rest of the story" we also find good news. Thank God, His mercy and power to forgive are even greater than our human sin and weakness. His love and kind providence are stronger than the terrible consequences of our fall.

WHEN STRENGTH BECOMES WEAKNESS

So far success had marked David's reign. He had triumphed over his enemies and had achieved his spiritual goal of bringing the ark to his capital. Now his nation enjoyed comparative peace and prosperity. Israel's king had brought his people to the very doorstep of fulfilling God's grand and noble purposes for their existence as a nation.

But sitting on the exalted heights of accomplishment presented a far greater jeopardy to David than had the most fearful perils when he fled from Saul. The king became dizzy with self-confidence, and the flattery and allurement of power and luxury. The influence of accepted social norms and attitudes, absorbed by his contact with the surrounding nations, led him to trust in his own wisdom, his own skill, and his own power.

"The cup most difficult to carry is not the cup that is empty, but the cup that is full to the brim. . . . It is prosperity that is most dangerous to spiritual life." [1]

Dizziness affects the sense of balance. It blurs vision, momentarily destroying focus and foresight, and often results in a fall. The brave David who had met Goliath "in the name of the Lord of hosts, the God of the armies of Israel" (1 Sam. 17:45) now settled into the false security of depending on his own military might and acumen. In the spring of the year when he should have led his army to the battlefront, he sent Joab and his other mighty men of valor to fight his battles for him. Why should he leave the comfort and luxury of his palace to march through the dust and gore of the battlefield?

"Then it happened one evening that David arose from his bed" (2 Sam. 11:2). Since it was only "evening" and not yet dark, he must have taken a long afternoon nap. He had time on his hands. Walking about on the palace roof, high above the surrounding houses, he could observe everything that transpired on the rooftops of the houses that crowded the steep slopes of the valleys that surrounded Jerusalem. (Even today, standing on the site of David's city, you can see the rows of rooftops in the nearby village of Silwan.) A woman performing her monthly bath of ritual purification caught his attention. Apparently having thoroughly absorbed the ancient attitude that "all things are permissible for the king," he "inquired about the woman" (verse 3).

He forgot his longings after righteousness, the joys of divine communion, and the close ties that had bound him to his God. In a moment of passion he made a choice that brought upon himself a cataract of calamities that followed him to the grave.

James, in the New Testament, gives us a definition of temptation, and a profile of sin's cause-effect relationship: "But a person is tempted when he is drawn away and trapped by his own evil desire. Then his evil desire conceives and gives birth to sin; and sin, when it is full-grown, gives birth to death" (James 1:14, 15, TEV). David would learn the full meaning of that principle.

Scripture describes Bathsheba as being a beautiful woman, but reveals virtually no insights into her character or her reactions or feelings toward the affair between them. Was the incident a strictly first time, accidental encounter? Or had her beauty already captivated David on some previous occasion? (Scripture does say he asked who she was, however.) Did she sense his desire for her? Had she in any way been seductive? Did she know that he could see her on her roof from the king's palace? Did she protest, when summoned by David's servants, that she was married? Did she lack the courage to resist? (See 1 Kings 1:11-17 for Bathsheba's reaction when someone threatened her son Solomon's right to the throne.) Did the king's command leave her any options? Or did she come willingly? Scripture silently veils the details. But the consequences of their secret rendezvous would not long remain silent! (2 Sam. 11:5).

SIN THAT REFUSES SECRECY

David must have been chagrined when he learned that she was pregnant. Quickly sending a message to Joab, he gave instructions that would hopefully cover his tracks. Bring Uriah back from the battlefront, to be at home with his wife so that when the child was born people would assume that it was just premature.

Uriah, one of David's most capable soldiers and called a Hittite (most probably an Aramaean from one of the Neo-Hittite states), accepted the Hebrew religion. (His name, meaning "Yahweh is my light," suggests that he may have been born in Israel.) A sense of duty to nation and God prevented him from enjoying the comforts of wife and home while his fellow soldiers risked their lives at the battlefront (verses 6-11).

His duplicity failing (verses 12, 13), David now resorted to the most cowardly of tactics to spare himself exposure. He who had refused to touch the Lord's anointed when the rules of warfare might have justified his taking Saul's life, he who had been repulsed by the revengeful assassinations of Abner and Ishbosheth, now stooped to murder an innocent and loyal subject in order to cover his own iniquity and protect his own royal reputation (see verses 14-21). Carrying his own death warrant back to the battlefront, Uriah became another victim of David's sin.

But David's greatest sin was not adultery and murder, vile as those moral lapses are. Rather he had prostituted the power and authority vested in him as Israel's ruler and protector of law and order. The king had used them instead for his own selfish and evil purposes. The biblical writer offers no excuses nor attempts to give any motivation as to why David committed adultery with Uriah's wife. Elsewhere the author is careful to explain anything that might be interpreted as wrongful behavior, but not here. He does nothing to reduce the shock of David's action.

The false premise that the ruler is somehow above the law that applies to his subjects, an attitude prevalent in the culture and time, tolerated the most heinous crimes in leaders that would have met swift retribution among their subjects. David had become the kind of ruler that 1 Samuel 8:11-17 warned against.

The influence of such an attitude in David lessened his own sense of sin, and created a credibility crisis with his family and subjects.

The monarch's sin had brought reproach on God. It had lessened the horror of sin in many minds, emboldened others in their transgressions, and generally weakened the national resolve to resist sin. For the honor of His name and for the sake of His people, God must intervene with measures to match the severity of the situation. The king's sin, though committed with the utmost secrecy, would have to be revealed and punished before the whole nation.

DAVID'S SIN EXPOSED

For about a year David had followed his course of deception, apparently unrepentant. Rumors and suspicions regarding his affair with Bathsheba had persisted. The sin he tried so hard to hide haunted him at every step.

When Bathsheba's period of mourning for Uriah ended, David had sent for her and "she became his wife. . . . But the thing that David had done displeased the Lord" (verse 27, KJV). The marginal reading suggests it "was evil in the eyes of" the Lord.

"Alas! how had the fine gold become dim! how had the most fine gold changed!" [2] One who had lived so close to his Maker, now brought reproach and dishonor on His holy name. Would Israel's second king follow the tragic footsteps of its first, persisting in rebellion and pride? Must God's promises to him now go unfulfilled? How would he respond if confronted with his sin? By denial, blame, and rationalization as had his predecessor? David now faced the most important choice of his life!

THE POOR MAN'S LAMB

Years before, at David's first anointing, the Lord had reminded Samuel that "the Lord does not see as man sees . . . , but the Lord looks at the heart" (1 Sam. 16:7). Grievous as was David's sin, the merciful, gracious, all-seeing God now sent the prophet Nathan to give David an opportunity to repent of his wrongdoing.

Appealing to David's concern for the poor and oppressed,

Nathan painted a word picture that would arouse the king's deepest emotions against injustice and inequity.

A rich man, with many flocks and herds, had robbed a poor man of the family's pet lamb, so as to prepare a meal for a traveler.

David's thoughts must have raced back to his boyhood. He saw his favorite pet lamb running around the house, collecting the head-rubbing and affection he had come to expect. Even now he felt his lamb's warm nose nudging against his bare leg. In his imagination he heard its pathetic bleating as a stranger took it away to an untimely death. The emotion of the story touched a nerve and captivated his conscience.

His anger was immediate and intense: "As the Lord lives, the man who has done this shall surely die! And he shall restore fourfold for the lamb, because he did this thing and because he had no pity" (2 Sam. 12:5, 6; cf. Ex. 22:1).

The king had pronounced his own death sentence. He deserved to die, having robbed, committed adultery, and been guilty of murder. (Both adultery and murder were punishable by death according to Leviticus 20:10 and Exodus 21:12-14.) But the prophet was not through. Looking David straight in the eye, and lifting his hand solemnly toward heaven, Nathan declared unflinchingly, "You are the man!"

Most kings, suffering such bold exposure, would have instantly commanded the execution of the meddlesome accuser. But David listened as the prophet continued his message from God: "I anointed you king over Israel, and I delivered you from the hand of Saul. I gave you your master's house . . . , and gave you the house of Israel and Judah. And if that had been too little, I also would have given you much more!" (2 Sam. 12:7, 8).

The prophet reminded him of his crime in killing Uriah, and stealing his wife for himself. Then the stinging words "Now therefore, the sword shall never depart from your house, because you have despised Me, and have taken the wife of Uriah the Hittite to be your wife. . . . Behold, I will raise up adversity against you from your own house; and I will take your wives before your eyes and give them to your neighbor. . . . For you did it secretly, but I will do this thing before all Israel, before the sun'' (verses 10-12).

DAVID'S REPENTANCE

During a long pause David, in stunned silence, allows the Spirit of God to speak to him. For a moment he forgets that he is king, forgets the royal luxury surrounding him, forgets the pride and passion that led to this encounter. All the guilt and bitter remorse that he had been deliberately suppressing, now suddenly bursts forth. "I have sinned against the Lord," he sobs (verse 13).

"When I kept silent, my bones grew old
Through my groaning all the day long.
For day and night Your hand was heavy upon me"
(Ps. 32:3, 4).

His repentance was no superficial "I'm sorry I got caught!" Rather, he sorrowed that he had sinned against the One he loved and worshiped:

"For I acknowledge my transgressions,
And my sin is ever before me.
Against You, You only, have I sinned,
And done this evil in Your sight" (Ps. 51:3, 4).

He saw himself in all of his sinfulness and degradation, recognized his sin in all of its enormity:

"Deliver me from bloodguiltiness, O God,
The God of my salvation" (verse 14).

"If You, Lord, should mark iniquities,
O Lord, who could stand?" (Ps. 130:3).

His only hope now rested in the One who could forgive and cleanse him of his sinfulness, and give him a new heart:

"Have mercy upon me, O God,
According to Your lovingkindness;
According to the multitude of Your tender mercies,
Blot out my transgressions.
Wash me thoroughly from my iniquity,
And cleanse me from my sin" (Ps. 51:1, 2).

"Purge me with hyssop, and I shall be clean;
Wash me, and I shall be whiter than snow" (verse 7).

"Create in me a clean heart, O God,
And renew a steadfast spirit within me" (verse 10).

He longed for the healing that only forgiveness can bring to a broken relationship:

"Hide Your face from my sins,
And blot out all my iniquities" (verse 9).

"Do not cast me away from Your presence,
And do not take Your Holy Spirit from me.
Restore to me the joy of Your salvation,
And uphold me with Your generous Spirit" (verses 11, 12).

David, recognizing how little he deserved and how much he owed, had offered the sacrifice God most desires:

"The sacrifices of God are a broken spirit,
A broken and a contrite heart—
These, O God, You will not despise" (verse 17).

THE HIGH COST OF SIN

Nathan encouraged the king with the assurance that "the Lord also has put away your sin; you shall not die. However, because by this deed you have given great occasion to the enemies of the Lord to blaspheme, the child also who is born to you shall surely die" (2 Sam. 12:13, 14).

David had pronounced a fourfold curse upon himself. Part 1 of the curse was now about to fall on him. For a whole week the repentant king pleaded with God to spare the innocent child from suffering his punishment. His family and attendants became concerned for his welfare when he refused either food or comfort. Finally, on the seventh day, the child died. His servants feared what he might do now. But upon hearing the news, he "arose from the ground, washed and anointed himself, and changed his clothes; and he went into the house of the Lord and worshiped" (verse 20).

Their king's calm response to the news amazed his servants. His answer reveals his ability to accept God's will. As long as the child lived there was hope. "But now he is dead; why should I fast? Can I bring him back again? I shall go to him, but he shall not return to me" (verse 23). Such resignation to God's will, the capacity to accept a "No" answer to our deepest heart longings, marks a mature faith that has been tested and tried in the fiery crucible of crisis and pain.

But David had sown to the wind (see Hosea 8:7). And now the whirlwind of tragedy swept through his own family with hurricane force. Part 2 of the fourfold curse involved incest in David's family. Amnon's rejection of his violated half sister, Tamar, led to his eventual murder by her brother Absalom and the latter's consequent exile and alienation (see 2 Sam. 13).

The sordid story repels us at every turn. Think of the heartsick agony, the remorse and grief that must have filled David's heart as he realized that one wrong choice, one moment of indulged passion, had brought a storm of violence into his own family. But his youngest son must have brightened the dark days of this period of his life.

JEDIDIAH

When David and Bathsheba's second son was born, they named him Solomon. But the Lord sent Nathan the prophet with a message, "so he called his name Jedidiah, because of the Lord" (2 Sam. 12:25). The name, meaning "beloved of Yahweh," was God's unique way of assuring David that he had been forgiven and accepted. Every time the king held his son in his arms, he found himself reminded of how tenderly and lovingly his own heavenly Father had dealt with him.

From both his pain of agony and the joy of his gratitude, David penned the words that have comforted and encouraged God's children through the ages:

"Out of the depths I have cried to You, O Lord;
   Lord, hear my voice!
   Let Your ears be attentive
   To the voice of my supplications.
   If You, Lord, should mark iniquities,
   O Lord, who could stand?
   But there is forgiveness with You,
   That You may be feared.
   I wait for the Lord, my soul waits,
   And in His word I do hope.
   My soul waits for the Lord

More than those who watch for the morning—
I say, more than those who watch for the morning.
O Israel, hope in the Lord;
For with the Lord there is mercy,
And with Him is abundant redemption.
And He shall redeem Israel
From all his iniquities'' (Ps. 130).

---

[1] *The Ministry of Healing,* p. 212.
[2] *Patriarchs and Prophets,* p. 720.

12

When the Creditor Collects

DEBIT ONE: SOUL PARALYSIS

In our credit card society almost anyone can buy on credit with one tiny piece of plastic. The temptation to indulge every whim with such ease proves the undoing of many people. The problem comes when eventually the creditor collects! And when not paid on time, the high interest on credit adds to the debt at an alarming rate. When people cannot meet it, or simply give up, they must file for bankruptcy.

Though forgiven, David now faced his creditors. So high was the interest on his debt that it took him the rest of his life to discharge it. Not because God willed it so, but because of the nature of evil. To his honor, David refused to succumb to bankruptcy. However, the story of his struggle with his spiritual debt takes up almost all of the rest of the book of Samuel.

Perhaps the most devastating effect of his debt was what it did to his buoyant and vivacious nature. The once-spirited David, who had faced lions, giants, and kings with courage, now seemed paralyzed by listlessness and irresolution. He who had led his people in worship with singing and sacred dance, now preferred retirement and solitude. His influence with his subjects weakened; he seemed incapable of governing with initiative and authority.

DEBIT TWO: FAMILY CALAMITY

His moral paralysis took its highest toll in his own family. Suffering the self-condemnation that sin inflicts on the emotional life of its victims, David failed to intervene with promptness and decisiveness in the series of crimes that erupted in his own household. The king's ability to make quick or crucial choices had been dealt an almost fatal blow.

When Amnon, David's firstborn son, raped his own half sister, the crime went unpunished and unrebuked. For two years Absalom, the full brother of the beautiful Tamar and her natural protector, witnessed her shattered spirit and emotional despair. Now rejected by the cruel Amnon and robbed of her dignity and virginity, "Tamar remained desolate in her brother Absalom's house" (2 Sam. 13:20).

The king, though outraged by the crime, seemed too paralyzed to deal with his selfish son. Absalom, seething with anger and revenge, waited to see what would happen. His father's negligence and apathy fueled his determination to take matters into his own hands. But he carefully concealed his feelings and plans for revenge.

His invitation to his father to attend the sheepshearing celebration (verses 24, 25) may suggest that he planned to kill both the king and Amnon, paving the way for him, as the heir apparent, to assert himself. Though David declined the invitation, he gave a somewhat reluctant permission for all the royal sons to attend, wondering, "Why should he [Amnon] go with you?" (verse 26). Did the king suspect his son's motives? Did a kind of fatherly premonition flash a warning to his now-weakened conscience?

Ironically, Absalom used the same tactic to accomplish his brother's demise as David used when he tried to cover his tracks with Uriah. He got his brothers drunk, and with their guards down, he gave the command "Strike Amnon!"

Pandemonium reigned as the rest of the king's sons fled in terror. Word reached David that all his sons had been slain. But the cunning Jonadab (verses 5, 32), who had helped Amnon plan his crime, now assured the king that Absalom had murdered only Amnon. Sobered and shocked, David, his family, and his court wept together for the fallen son and brother. Part 3 of David's curse, in all its ugliness, had shattered his life.

DEBIT THREE: EXILE AND ALIENATION

Meanwhile, Absalom fled to Geshur in Syria to seek refuge with his mother's family. David had sinned in marrying Maacah, the pagan princess from Geshur, and had set a precedent that God had specifically warned against. Israel's kings were not to add wives, a status symbol both of royal power and a means of establishing diplomatic ties with other nations, much less pagan women who would lead them away from God.

David's fondness for his erring son and his negligence in dealing with Amnon now prevented him from taking immediate action to bring Absalom to justice. In a kind of compromise, David refused to allow him to return to Jerusalem. Alienated and cut off from participating in national affairs, Absalom continued to seethe with anger against his father and to scheme for revenge.

The record does not state that he appealed to his cousin Joab for help in effecting a reconciliation, but he likely did. Finding a woman of great wisdom and tact, Joab sent her to the king as a widow who sought pardon for her only surviving son who had murdered his brother.

David quickly detected the ruse. "Is the hand of Joab with you in all this?" (2 Sam. 14:19). Admitting Joab's involvement, she appealed to the king. "To bring about this change of affairs your servant Joab has done this thing; but my lord is wise, according to the wisdom of the angel of God" (verse 20).

The king conceded to Joab's wishes, commanding that the exiled son be brought back to Jerusalem, but refusing to see him, a choice both of them would live to regret.

DEBIT FOUR: CONSPIRACY AND REVENGE

For two years the handsome and dashing young prince lived in Jerusalem with his family of three sons and one daughter (named Tamar for her aunt, who also resided with them, and kept alive the memory of the tragedy). But not once did he visit his father. Imagine living in the same town (Jerusalem was only a few acres in size) and having no contact with your own father, or son, or your grandchildren! Consider the range of emotions that would jostle against one another every time you almost had an accidental encounter.

David had erred in allowing him to return to Jerusalem, yet not see him. A man of Absalom's ambitious, impulsive, and scheming character could not do other than foment dissatisfaction against the king. His commanding appearance and charisma made him a hero, not an offender, in popular opinion.

The king loved his gifted son, but too late he saw the evil effects of his lack of discipline. Now his attempts to teach him a lesson and set an example before the people only magnified the problem. Too much damage had been done, too many bad feelings generated.

When Joab refused to come at Absalom's request, the prince sent his servants to set the military commander's neighboring fields on fire. Absalom's demand to see the king had its origin in his desire to enhance his personal chances for the throne. Somehow, though, Joab managed to bring the two together in a kind of mock reconciliation.

DEBIT FIVE: REBELLION AND A COUP D'ETAT

Now officially restored to royal favor, Absalom began his active campaign to win the hearts of the people. David's paralysis had permeated his administration of justice. A tendency to negligence and delay now seemed to characterize his rule. Stationing himself at the city gate, the regular place to hear and decide lawsuits, Absalom listened to their grievances and decried the fact that "there is no deputy of the king to hear you. . . . 'Oh, that I were made judge in the land, and everyone who has any suit or cause would come to me; then I would give him justice' " (2 Sam. 15:3, 4).

For several years the cunning prince "stole the hearts of the men of Israel" (verse 6), that is, deceived or duped the people's affections (cf. Genesis 31:20), and he fomented discontent against the government. He built his support on the growing frustration with David's rule and the thousands of grievances that exist among the people of any nation. With the pomp and ceremony appropriate to a king, Absalom would ride into the city with his flashing chariots and regal horses. (Besides surrounding himself with royal trappings, he ignored the fact that God had forbidden His people to use horses and chariots, the mechanized weapons of the ancient world, because they were to depend on Him for defense instead; see Psalm 20:7.) Though feigning a love for justice and identifying with the role of king as royal judge, Absalom had already demonstrated that he lived by a spirit of revenge, not righteous principles. Yet David's affection for his popular son blinded him to his scheming. And when Absalom requested permission to go to Hebron [1] to pay a religious vow, David sent him with his blessing, comforted by his son's evidence of piety, but completely oblivious to the fact that a conspiracy against his throne had now reached its peak. Hebron had once been David's seat of power as well as the prince's hometown, and Absalom wanted to take advantage of that historical fact.

So cunningly had Absalom laid his plans that some of the leading citizens of Jerusalem, supposing they were going on a religious pilgrimage, "went along innocently and did not know anything" (2 Sam. 15:11). But Ahithophel, one of David's chief counselors, gladly accepted the formal invitation to join the rebellion. He no doubt had been instrumental in helping to plan the revolt, venting his personal vendetta against the king for the disgrace done to the family through Bathsheba, his granddaughter. [2] His acclaimed reputation for wisdom now gave credibility and power to Absalom's cause. "The conspiracy grew strong, for the people with Absalom continually increased in number" (verse 12). All the mistakes David had made in his rule now reaped their consequences.

When word of the rebellion reached David at Jerusalem, he reacted with shock. How could his son whom he loved so much become traitor and perhaps even murderer of his own father? How could he have planned a revolt so well, right at the palace gate, without word of it leaking out?

Shaking the deep depression that had so long paralyzed him, David now responded with the energy and spirit of earlier years as he prepared to meet the terrible emergency. With Absalom mustering his forces at Hebron, only about 20 miles away, the rebels would soon be entering the gates of Jerusalem.

What thoughts must have raced through the king's mind as he looked out over his beautiful capital? Should he maintain his right to the throne and defend the city, bringing the carnage of battle into it and possibly endangering the holy ark? Or should he flee, hoping for help from those who still remained loyal to him, and trusting to the mercy of God?

"So David said to all his servants . . . , 'Arise, and let us flee. . . . Make haste to depart, lest he overtake us suddenly and bring disaster upon us, and strike the city with the edge of the sword' " (verse 14). Would all that he had worked so hard to build and establish, now be left to the reckless insurgents? With a breaking heart, David left his beloved capital, trusting it and himself to God.

In a funeral-like procession, David led the way, flanked by his loyal bodyguards—among them Ittai the Gittite, who insisted on accompanying him. The priests carried the ark of the covenant, and faithful counselors and subjects followed behind. He had exchanged his royal robes for sackcloth, the symbol of mourning. The rocky floor of the Kidron Valley stung his bare feet. His smarting conscience reminded him of the sins that had brought him to this moment. He wept as he climbed the steep ascent up the slope of the Olives (probably the second of the three summits of the Mount of Olives). His only hope now—the mercy and longsuffering of his God!

A thousand years later, David's Son, the Saviour of the world, would make His way across that same Kidron Valley, up the same Mount of Olives to the Garden of Gethsemane. There He would agonize not over His own sins, but those of David His human ancestor, and the sins of every child of God. There He would cry out, "Let this cup pass . . . nevertheless, not My will, but Thine be done!"

Though comforted momentarily by the presence of the ark, David's concern for the glory of God prompted him to send the priests back with the sacred chest. "Carry the ark of God back into the city. If I find favor in the eyes of the Lord, He will bring me back and show me both it and His habitation" (verse 25).

DEBIT SIX: TREACHERY AND DEATH

When Hushai the Archite came to meet the king to offer his services, David wisely sent him back to the city to "defeat the counsel of Ahithophel" (v. 34). The refugee king well knew that the crafty advice of his once trusted counselor could now prove his undoing and Absalom's success.

David's fears were not without cause. Ahithophel, desiring to ingratiate himself to the new king and burn the bridges to any possible reconciliation between father and son, now advised him to publicly show his authority by taking over the king's harem (a common custom in those days). Possession of the harem would provide a form of legitimacy to Absalom's claim to the throne. The prince pitched his tent on the roof, perhaps the very balcony where David had stood when he made his fatal choice so many years before. Another part of the curse had reached its fulfillment: "You did it secretly, but I will do this thing before all Israel" (2 Sam. 12:12).

Hushai's arrival at the palace pleased the usurper. Seeking a second opinion on Ahithophel's plan of attack to overtake David and his men, Absalom now asked Hushai for his advice. Providentially, he accepted Hushai's suggestion, fulfilling David's hopes. Totally devastated by the turn of events, Ahithophel took his own life. Meanwhile, David used the time to cross the Jordan and organize the now-increasing number of loyalists at Mahanaim, Saul's old capital. Hushai had bought for him the precious time needed to meet the emergency.

Though popular with the masses, Absalom had never spent a day in battle, and was ill-prepared to meet his father's trained forces. David now divided his men into three companies under his ablest commanders, and prepared to lead them in battle. But the people insisted that he not go along, indicating their great love and respect for him: "But you are worth ten thousand of us now" (2 Sam. 18:3). David deferred to their wishes.

The refugee king sent his forces into the rough wooded hills of Ephraim, possibly an area east of the Jordan. Even after centuries of deforestation, there are dense patches of scrubby forest south of the Jabbok River in the modern country of Jordan. During a Palestine Liberation Organization revolt against Jordan's king Hussein during the 1970s, the PLO forces hid in the dense growth there. Unable to capture the PLO troops in the rough terrain, the Jordanian military firebombed the forests to drive the rebels out.

Absalom's poorly organized forces with their horses and chariots would be hard put to fight in such rugged terrain against David's troops who had experience in guerrilla warfare.

The prince's arrogance and vanity followed him to the battlefront. Astride a mule (the Israelite symbol of royalty), Absalom rode unwittingly into his death trap, probably a terebinth tree. Tradition says that he caught his hair in some branches, but Scripture does not mention his hair, and Ellen White states only that his head was caught in the wide-spreading branches of a tree. [3] Perhaps he wedged his head in a forked branch, and the mule ran out from under him, leaving him suspended in the air.

David's last words to his military commanders had been, "Deal gently for my sake with the young man Absalom" (verse 5). But the hard-boiled Joab was in no mood for sentimental feelings. This was war, the king's throne was at stake, and a nation's welfare hung in the balance. Did the king care more about his rebellious son than he did even his army and people? With three stabs through Absalom's heart, the revolt came to an inglorious end. Joab blew the trumpet, calling a halt to the pursuit. In contempt and disgust, he threw the once handsome body into a pit, covering it with a pile of rocks, certainly not the kind of monument the fallen prince had envisioned or planned for himself. The burial Absalom received was that reserved for an accursed man (cf. Joshua 7:26; 8:29; 10:27). He who had sought to ascend to the throne had instead literally gone into the pit.

The rebellion was over. The nation had escaped the terrible prospect of a long, drawn-out civil war. But was it a time for rejoicing? Hardly! Ahimaaz, son of Zadok the priest, begged to take the tidings to the king of "how the Lord has avenged him of his enemies" (2 Sam. 18:19). But Joab knew all too well David's intense love for his erring son. He appointed a Cushite to carefully bear the news. Ahimaaz outran him and reached David first, but he hedged on the message. "I saw a great tumult, but

I did not know what it was about'' (verse 29).

David's sorrow knew no bounds. "O my son Absalom—my son, my son Absalom—if only I had died in your place!'' (verse 33). Joab had no patience with the king's personal loss and grief. A whole nation might have perished in the encounter, and thousands of lives had been sacrificed to protect the king and his kingdom. Now David seemed oblivious to everything except his grief over his dead son. Those who had fought so valiantly for him now slipped away, feeling like losers instead of victors. The army was almost on the point of desertion. Then Joab intervened. The military commander spared no words in his reproof, warning his king that unless he recognized what his followers had done for him, he would meet a fate worse than any that had ever befallen him before (verse 7).

DAVID'S CREDITS

Quickly David rallied and heeded the counsel of his commander in chief. Sitting at the gate in view of the people, he brought the much-needed assurance that he appreciated their efforts.

He had paid heavily the debts he owed. But through all his ordeal he had also built some credits. David's greatness—his spirit of humility and willingness to listen to the advice of those under his command—had saved the day.

But even more important, in his adversity the king had grown in his dependence on his God. When every earthly support had crumpled beneath him, he grasped the hand that alone could save him. In the dark night of his flight from Jerusalem, he had moved from the agony of grief to the repose of trust!

"Lord, how they have increased who trouble me!
Many are they who rise up against me.
Many are they who say of me,
'There is no help for him in God.'
But You, O Lord, are a shield for me;
My glory and the One who lifts up my head.
I cried to the Lord with my voice,
And He heard me from His holy hill.
I lay down and slept;

I awoke, for the Lord sustained me.
I will not be afraid of ten thousands of people
Who have set themselves against me all around''
    (Ps. 3:1-6).

---

[1] The rendering in 2 Samuel 15:7 of ''forty years'' should read ''four,'' as it does in some manuscripts.

[2] See *Patriarchs and Prophets*, p. 735.

[3] *Ibid.*, p. 743.

When the Rock Speaks

THE REAL DAVID

The legendary King David, loved and lauded by his people through the centuries of Jewish history, looms larger than life. Jews are fascinated by him, adore him, name their children for him, and claim him as the central figure of their heritage. Christians love David, delight in stories about him, and revere him as the progenitor of the Messiah. Peoples of other races admire him, some seeking to find their roots in his dynasty. [1]

Yet the Samuel narrative seems relentless in its effort to reveal the painful truth about him, showing us his life in all its rawness and incongruity. Even the closing chapters of the book, which we might hope would end on a more positive note, wade through more of his mistakes and blunders in an almost postscriptlike commentary (as though not enough had yet been told). Why? Why must the author of Samuel depict the truth about this great man so brutally, so close up, almost to the point of magnifying it?

At least two reasons seem evident. The first has to do with our human tendency to idolize and worship our heroes. The Word of God sizes up people as they really are, not as we would like to idealize them. So the book of Samuel clearly reveals David as a man of passions, weaknesses, faults, inconsistencies, and glaring defects. This aspect of his portrayal sometimes overshadows his magnanimity of character and his royal accomplishments.

The second reason, as we have noted before, is that the story of David is that of humanity itself. It is the tragic account of the human dilemma: the sordid and complex mess we call life. If David is as bad as all that, why does God bother with him? Why does He bother with any of us, for that matter? Is there any hope for us?

And the story of David comes resounding down the corridors of time with the glorious answer: yes, there is hope! In spite of our deficiencies, in spite of our failures, in spite of our sinfulness, there is hope. But not because we deserve it. Not because we are who we are. Rather because God is who He is! Because we choose to respond to Him!

The fundamental message of David's life is that he consistently chose to cast himself on God's mercy. No matter how badly he failed at times, no matter how difficult his trials, or how severe the discipline he suffered, David always came back to God—the one solid, secure, and stable point in his often hectic life.

"My soul, wait silently for God alone,
   For my expectation is from Him.
   He only is my rock and my salvation; . . .
   In God is my salvation and my glory;
   The rock of my strength,
   And my refuge, is in God" (Ps. 62:5-7).
"From the end of the earth I will cry to You,
   When my heart is overwhelmed;
   Lead me to the rock that is higher than I" (Ps. 61:2).
"To You I will cry, O Lord my Rock.
   Do not be silent to me,
   Lest, if You are silent to me,
   I become like those who go down to the pit" (Ps. 28:1).

David's confidence in his spiritual Rock, his eagerness to know His will, to hear Him speak, to follow His guidance, endeared him to the heart of God and to the hearts of His people forever.

FRIENDS AND ENEMIES

Israel's king had learned through the long, storm-tossed years of his life to hear God speak through different voices. Sometimes even through an enemy. Such had been the case when David fled from Jerusalem. Shimei, a relative of Saul, had followed him along the hillside, cursing him, hurling stones and insults at the ruler fleeing into exile. The warrior Abishai, David's nephew and Joab's brother, wanted to behead him for his accusations, but David patiently deferred. "Let him curse. Maybe the Lord is trying to tell me something through him" (see 2 Sam. 16:5-13). After Absalom's death Shimei approached David with an apology. Again Abishai wanted him put to death. Once more David graciously pardoned him (but cf. 1 Kings 2:8, 9). He could leave the work of judgment to the righteous God, the just judge, "who tests the hearts and minds." He need not defend himself, for he knew that "my defense is of God" (Ps. 7:9-11).

The Lord had ministered to David during his exile from Jerusalem through his friends. Barzillai the Gileadite had supplied food and other provisions for the ruler and his followers while they camped at Mahanaim (2 Sam. 17:27-29). In a gesture of appreciation David now offered the wealthy chieftain a place in the royal city (2 Sam. 19:31-39). Though Barzillai declined, the touching farewell between the two men reveals David's human tenderness and generosity. He did not neglect or forget to repay kindness with gratitude and appreciation.

RESTORATION OF THE KINGDOM

Though the rebellion had been crushed by the death of Absalom, the affairs of state remained in disarray and its subjects torn by rivalry and tribal factions. David did not immediately assume the throne, but waited to see what the people would do. The tribe of Judah responded first, escorting the king across the Jordan. The men of the northern tribes were furious and jealously accused the Judahites of trying to steal away their king. The two factions now became embroiled in petty bickering and disputes. The king must somehow bring them together.

In a quick diplomatic move the king made Amasa, former commander of Absalom's rebel army, his own chief of staff in place of Joab. He no doubt hoped by this action to placate the angry northern tribes.

Meanwhile, Sheba, a Benjamite, took adv
animosity between the tribes, and triggered a
David. Joab quickly squelched the rebellion, but no.
had succeeded in murdering his rival, Amasa. Whatever hope
David may have had for a reprieve from the ruthless and powerful
Joab now faded into acceptance.

Eventually peace returned to Israel. David once again established his rule. Second Samuel 20 records David's cabinet: Joab,
commander of his army; Benaiah, in charge of the royal
bodyguards; Adoram supervised the labor force; Jehoshaphat was
herald; Sheva, scribe; Zadok and Abiathar, priests; and Ira, chief
minister or private priest. David had a high regard for the men
who assisted him in government, and especially for his military
officials. A list of his mighty men and their deeds takes up almost
a whole chapter (2 Sam. 23).

MORE CHOICES AND CALAMITIES

The story of the famine and the Gibeonite affair sounds
strange and offensive to our Western minds. But it must be
understood, if not justified, in its cultural setting. When a
drought persisted for three years, David "inquired of the Lord"
(2 Sam. 21:1). He learned that there was a blood-guilt upon the
house of Saul because he had killed the Gibeonites, an incident
apparently not recorded in Scripture, though some have tried to
identify it with the slaughter of the priests at Nob (1 Sam.
22:6-23).

The Gibeonites were not originally related to Israel by blood,
but were protected by a treaty (see Joshua 9) that Saul had
flagrantly violated when he apparently massacred a large number
of them in cold blood. The remaining Gibeonites, not satisfied
with financial compensation, their only legal recourse, now
demanded full revenge, blood for blood upon Saul's house.
David must have winced at the thought. Yet his sense of justice
and pledge of honor demanded that he make amends to this
wronged ethnic group.

Among the seven descendants of Saul who were hanged, five
were sons of Merab, whom tradition says that Michal (Saul's
daughter and David's wife) had raised for her sister, who had

evidently died (cf. 2 Sam. 21:8 with 1 Sam. 18:17-19; and 2 Sam. 3:13-16). Whatever emotional feelings David may have had in all of this, he showed his respect to the house of Saul by giving them an honorable burial.

Though the Philistines were not a major threat during most of David's reign, they were troublesome enough to ensure that the swords of Israel's army did not rust for lack of use. David had been a valiant soldier and a skilled military leader. In one of their skirmishes with the Philistines, the king nearly lost his life except for the quick intervention of his nephew Abishai. From that point on, his men insisted that he not go to battle with them, "lest you quench the lamp of Israel" (2 Sam. 21:17).

Few men can handle adulation, praise, honor, and power as well as David did. His simple childhood as a shepherd, his years of wilderness exile and hiding from Saul, his communion with God and nature, his poetic inclination and deep faith in God, helped prepare him for the glorious reign that was his. Yet honor, success, prestige, and temporal riches still had their impact on David, making him susceptible to worldly influences.

David planned to increase the size of his already-powerful armed forces by a military draft. He now ordered a census. Even Joab protested the rash and unnecessary action. But the king was adamant. The Samuel account says that God in anger moved David to number Israel, a pattern found in the earlier parts of the Old Testament where the writer attributes whatever happens to God's sovereignty, whether it be either good or bad (cf., for example, Ex. 4:11). The parallel account in Chronicles suggests that "Satan stood up against Israel, and moved David to number Israel" (1 Chron. 21:1). While David's action may have resulted from personal pride and ambition, the context suggests that God also may have used the occasion to punish His people for their sins. [2] "Nevertheless the king's word prevailed against Joab and . . . the captains of the army" (2 Sam. 24:4).

Under the theocracy, God was the defender and protector of His people. The Lord had warned Israel that one of the dangers of a monarchy would be military conscription. Their human sovereigns would oppress them, demanding their sons to enhance their own political and military power. Now David was fulfilling that prophecy. And if David, the greatest of Israel's kings, succumbed to such a temptation, what could Israel expect in the days to come, when the reign of "evil" men would be the rule, not the exception?

Hardly had the results of the census come in when "David's heart condemned him." Convicted of his sin, he begged God for forgiveness, "for I have done very foolishly" (verse 10). It takes courage and humility for a man in his position to admit to a wrong policy, especially one for which he had been so adamant.

David had made a wrong choice. Now the prophet Gad, David's seer, came to him with three choices—three forms of punishment for his sin. Distressed by the prospects of once again becoming a victim of his own sins and bringing suffering upon his people, David pleaded, "Please let us fall into the hand of the Lord, for His mercies are great" (verse 14).

The terrible plague did its devastating work as in a short time thousands of men of military age died. But when the destroying angel reached Jerusalem, "the Lord relented."

The king's touching appeal to God again shows his spirit of humility and genuine repentance: "Surely I have sinned, and I have done wickedly; but these sheep, what have they done?" (verse 17).

David saw the death angel above the threshing floor of Araunah the Jebusite. Immediately he negotiated to purchase the property so that he might build an altar. There on Mount Moriah, where tradition says that more than 800 years before Abraham had offered up his son Isaac, David "offered burnt offerings and peace offerings." There on that same spot his son Solomon would someday erect a beautiful Temple to the glory of God.

"So the Lord heeded the prayers for the land, and the plague was withdrawn from Israel" (verse 25). A strange ending for the book of Samuel? Not really, for it is a portrait of redemption, the foreshadowing of the salvation to come!

THE LEGACY OF DAVID

While the book of Samuel spends considerable time on David's personal life, Scripture leaves the record of his many accomplishments to the book of 1 Chronicles. Israel's greatest king was a statesman of keen administrative ability. In spite of setbacks such as war and his own family problems, he managed to accumulate great wealth during his reign. As a nation, Israel would never again reach the pinnacle of wealth, splendor, and glory that it enjoyed during the time of David and Solomon. Never again would the power and extent of David's empire be fully equaled.

King David had desired to build a house for his God. But the Lord denied him the honor because his hands had been stained by bloodshed. But he dedicated his energies to planning and preparing for his son to construct the Temple. He gathered silver and gold, precious stones, fine cedar and acacia wood from Lebanon, huge precut golden-hued stones from the local limestone quarries, and a temple fund that staggers the imagination.

David organized the priests and Levites for the Temple service, writing hymns and prayers for worship. He left to Israel perhaps its richest heritage of poetry and music of all time.

The psalms of David, therefore, and the Psalter that he began to compile, are without question his greatest legacy to the world. God's people through the ages have been blessed and ministered to by his songs and prayers.

"The psalms of David pass through the whole range of experience, from the depths of conscious guilt and self-condemnation to the loftiest faith and the most exalted communing with God. [3] They will live on to bless God's children as long as time shall last and into the great beyond!

WHEN THE ROCK SPEAKS

In his last words, David testified:
"The Spirit of the Lord spoke by me,
  And His word was on my tongue.
  The God of Israel said,
  The Rock of Israel spoke to me" (2 Sam. 23:2).

What did David hear when the Rock spoke to him? The Lord declared, "I am the Good Shepherd," and he responded with a song of confidence: "The Lord is my Shepherd; I shall not want."

But as Christians we can hear even more clearly than Israel's king could. Through David's words we can hear the Rock speak to the Father, saying:

"I delight to do Your will, O my God,
And Your law is within my heart" (Ps. 40:8).

In David's psalms we can hear a lonely, forlorn voice, somewhere between Gethsemane and Calvary, suffering in our place:

"You have laid me in the lowest pit,
In darkness, in the depths.
Your wrath lies heavy upon me,
And You have afflicted me with all Your waves.
You have put my acquaintances far from Me"
(Ps. 88:6-8).

David enables us to hear the Rock cry out as He hung suspended between heaven and earth on a cruel cross:

"My God, My God, why have You forsaken Me?
Why are You so far from helping Me?" (Ps. 22:1).

"Many bulls have surrounded Me;
Strong bulls of Bashan have encircled Me.
They gape at Me with their mouths,
As a raging and roaring lion" (verse 12).

"The assembly of the wicked has enclosed Me.
They pierced My hands and My feet;
I can count all My bones.
They look and stare at Me.
They divide My garments among them,
And for My clothing they cast lots" (verses 16, 17).

And then through David's inspired words comes the cry of resignation:

"Into Your hand I commit my spirit" (Ps. 31:5).

We can hear the Rock assert, as He faced the prospects of a cold tomb:

"For You will not leave my soul in Sheol,
Nor will You allow Your Holy One to see corruption"
(Ps. 16:10).

David also brings us the triumphant note of victory:

"The Lord said to my Lord,
'Sit at My right hand,

Till I make Your enemies Your footstool.'
The Lord shall send the rod of Your strength out of Zion.
Rule in the midst of Your enemies!'' (Ps. 110:1, 2).

And because David listened to the Rock, he could say of Him:

"Blessed be the Lord my Rock" (Ps. 144:1).

"The Lord is gracious and full of compassion,
Slow to anger and great in mercy,
The Lord is good to all,
His tender mercies are over all His works" (Ps. 145:8, 9).

Israel's shepherd-king invites all who trust in the Rock to join him in a chorus of praise:

"Let them praise the name of the Lord,
For His name alone is exalted;
His glory is above the earth and heaven" (Ps. 148:13).

"Let everything that has breath praise the Lord,
Praise the Lord!" (Ps. 150:6).

In his closing words David expressed the ideal reign the Rock had desired for him:

"He who rules over men must be just,
Ruling in the fear of God.
And he shall be like the light of the morning . . .
Like the tender grass springing out of the earth . . ."

Then he adds:

"Although my house is not so with God,
Yet He has made with me an everlasting covenant"
(2 Sam. 23:3-5).

"Great had been David's fall, but deep was his repentance, ardent was his love, and strong his faith. He had been forgiven much, and therefore he loved much. (Luke 7:48)." [4]

As a symbol of His covenant love, God had graciously turned tragedy into triumph when He chose Solomon to be David's successor. The son whom the prophet named "Jedidiah, because of the Lord," or beloved of the Lord (2 Sam. 12:25), would remind the king to his dying day that God's mercy was greater than his sin, His ability to heal stronger than his sickness, and His power to restore bigger than his brokenness.

Jedidiah! We too may be "beloved of the Lord." We too may

choose to accept the Rock and His gracious covenant mercy. For, we, like David, are never far from grace:

"Your mercy, O Lord, will hold me up.
In the multitude of my anxieties within me,
Your comforts delight my soul. . . .
The Lord has been my defense,
And my God the Rock of my refuge" (Ps. 94:18-22).
"Happy is he who has the God of Jacob for his help,
Whose hope is in the Lord his God" (Ps. 146:5).

---

[1] Ethiopian tradition claimed that its former royal family was descended from David through the queen of Sheba and a son born to her as a result of her visit to Solomon in Jerusalem.

[2] See *Patriarchs and Prophets*, p. 748.

[3] *Ibid.*, p. 754.

[4] *Ibid.*

trepidation - nervous - fear

liturgy - Different churches use different forms of worship

Samuel's sons was dishonest page 30

Do not go along with the world page 33

Saul father ever rich 36

Saul was good.

Appendix

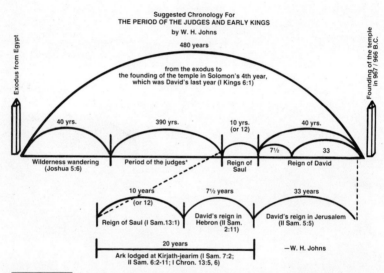

Suggested Chronology For
THE PERIOD OF THE JUDGES AND EARLY KINGS
by W. H. Johns

Exodus from Egypt

Founding of the temple in 967 / 966 B.C.

480 years

from the exodus to
the founding of the temple in Solomon's 4th year,
which was David's last year (I Kings 6:1)

40 yrs.   390 years.   10 yrs. (or 12)   40 yrs.

7½   33

Wilderness wandering (Joshua 5:6)   Period of the judges*   Reign of Saul   Reign of David

10 years (or 12)   7½ years   33 years

Reign of Saul (I Sam.13:1)   David's reign in Hebron (II Sam. 2:11)   David's reign in Jerusalem (II Sam. 5:5)

20 years

Ark lodged at Kirjath-jearim (I Sam. 7:2; II Sam. 6:2-11; I Chron. 13:5, 6)

—W. H. Johns

---

*Figure of 390 obtained from adding all the years in the following texts: Judges 3:8, 11, 14, 30; 4:3; 5:31; 6:1; 8:28; 9:22; 10:2, 3, 7-8; 12:7, 9, 11, 14; 13:1 (2 SDA BC, 127). Samson and Eli ruled Israel during the 40 years of Philistine oppression (Judges 15:20; I Sam. 4:18; 7:13).